VECINO

Training Division, CPO (L-24)
Military Sealift Command, Atlantic
Military Ocean Terminal, Bldg. 42
Bayonne, New Jersey 07002

THE SECRETS OF
SUCCESSFUL
PROJECT
MANAGEMENT

THE SECRETS OF
SUCCESSFUL
PROJECT
MANAGEMENT

Ralph L. Kliem
with Alexander Hamilton Institute

A Wiley Press Book
John Wiley & Sons, Inc.
New York • Chichester • Brisbane • Toronto • Singapore

Publisher: Stephen Kippur
Editor: Elizabeth G. Perry
Managing Editor: Katherine S. Bolster
Editing, Design, and Production: Publication Services

Library of Congress Cataloging-in-Publication Data

The secrets of successful project management.

  1. Industrial project management.   I. Alexander Hamilton Institute (U.S.)
T56.8.S43   1986   658.4'04   86-5567
ISBN 0-471-83670-2

Printed in the United States of America

86 87 10 9 8 7 6 5 4 3 2 1

CONTENTS

FOREWORD

There are many books on project management. Most of them address the subject on a theoretical level; that is, their coverage is so esoteric that many managers, supervisors, and professional employees find it difficult to apply the concepts to their immediate working environment. In *The Secrets of Successful Project Management*, the author deliberately avoids the theoretical approach, and instead presents practical, how-to information on ways to plan, organize, and control any project.

This book is written from the perspective of a project manager for one important reason. Project managers are the "doers" of a project. That is, they are responsible for actually planning, organizing, and controlling a project. From their vantage point, you can learn, step-by-step, how to manage a project from its inception.

This book is meant for two levels of readers. Supervisors, managers, and professional employees in any industry who know little or nothing of project management will find this book beneficial. Not only will they see how a project is managed by a project manager, they will have forms, checklists, and worksheets that they can use for their own project. Readers who already have some experience in project management will also find the book useful as a guide. The checklists, forms, and worksheets will give them ideas to incorporate in the management of their own projects.

A construction project was chosen for the case study because such projects are the easiest to understand. The activities are easier to define—many people can visualize somewhat in their minds how a building is constructed, and the final product is something all readers can relate to. The book, however, is not applicable only to the construction industry. The techniques for constructing network diagrams, developing effective communication systems, and monitoring resource utilization and costs are applicable to projects in all industries, whether data processing, insurance, aerospace, manufacturing, or construction.

The recent experience on many fronts with motivating workers, a new sensitivity to their needs for a feeling of participation and ownership of responsibilities and commitments is an entire subject in itself. Because it is, this book is confined to the *tools* of sound project management. Readers should keep in mind, however, that the human factor is the key to a successful project of any kind, and that to enlist this human support by communication (two-way), reinforcement and feedback is the project manager's primary task.

1

THE ROLE OF THE PROJECT MANAGER

A project is a major undertaking for any company, large or small. Capital, labor and often property will be invested in it, and a successful outcome can never be a foregone conclusion.

It is only sensible, therefore, to make every effort to ensure the success of any project that is contemplated: plan ahead as carefully as possible for every aspect of the work, try to avoid problems before they arise, have everything as well organized in advance as it is possible to be. Although such precautions will not absolutely guarantee the success of the venture, taking them will go a long way toward making it successful—and failure to take them is almost sure to result in failure of the project.

And whose responsibility is it to see that these plans and precautions are actually carried out? The individual in charge—the project manager. While he or she will have a staff and will make a serious effort to obtain and hold the participation and cooperation of every person on the project, the final responsibility for planning, organizing and controlling the venture lies in the hands of the project manager. As soon as a company makes the decision to undertake a project, the project manager should be appointed and given the authority to make the decisions that are vital for launching and completing a successful project. To have responsibility without the necessary authority to carry out that responsibility makes the responsibility meaningless and the task a blind alley.

Whatever the project is—the construction of a building, the implementation of a data processing program, the launching of a new product, the expansion of a sales effort—the project manager has the same general functions: *planning, organizing* and *controlling* the work. How does the project manager go about fulfilling these functions? While any good manager has a feeling for the job at hand, and will develop ways to analyze and systematize the work to be done, the tools described in this book should make it easier to do this with top efficiency and effectiveness.

Below is a brief outline of the project manager's key responsibilities, which are, not coincidentally, also the basic requirements of a successfully completed project. In the chapters that follow, each of these will be discussed in detail, with descriptions of the methodology to carry them out.

THE PROJECT MANAGER'S KEY RESPONSIBILITIES

Define Goals

Clearly define the goals and objectives of the project, so that not only the manager but everyone involved with it has a clear, specific picture of what these goals and objectives are. If all the employees know what they are working toward, they will not only perform more productively, but will be able to feel that they are truly part of the effort and that the goals and objectives are not just management's, but their own.

It is a good idea to prepare a written version of the project objectives; putting them on paper will force a clear and specific definition, and will be a way to communicate them to everyone involved. It is an even better idea to arrive at this definition at a meeting of the people who are to be working on the project. Their input will be invaluable and their enhanced sense of participation a big factor in the success of the venture.

Schedule Each Task

After goals are defined, it is important, again ideally with the people who are to work on the project, to express them in terms of specific tasks, and to break the tasks down into a cohesive schedule and plan. While this cannot be done wholly in conference with the staff and employees, some general beginning can be made together that will then be elaborated and detailed by the project manager (as we will describe in a later chapter). This action will help the employees to have a clear idea of what their individual responsibilities are. They will know what contribution they must make to the successful completion of the project, and will feel that they are working with a direction, rather than aimlessly.

Estimate Costs

It is the project manager's job to develop accurate financial estimates for doing the project, both in detail for discrete sections of the work and for the total project. In doing this, it is important that the data used is the most up-to-date and that the project manager be aware of the possibility of price increases in materials and labor, of the time value of money and of the continuous changing character of a free market economy. Not only must the financial data be up-to-date and accurate, it should be as full and relevant as possible. Estimates based on scanty, insignificant or irrelevant data will not be realistic and could cause enormous cost overruns and other problems once the project is under way. It is vital to guard against *avoidable* cost overruns and possible to save thousands of dollars by doing so. (Some cost overruns are unavoidable: unforeseen labor shortages and escalating material costs are not within the control of the project manager.)

Schedule Carefully

When scheduling, allow enough time to complete the project properly. While it is true that many projects are set up with built-in time constraints, it is important to be as realistic as possible about this. A manufacturing firm may want to deliver an item to the market before a competitor does, but if the rush to market results in a product that is inferior, its manufacture prohibitively costly, or its existence forced to depend on the misallocation of resources, the hoped-for advantage of early completion becomes a severe disadvantage.

Allocate Resources

The project manager has the best overall view of the project, and it is therefore his or her job to allocate the resources of machinery, material and labor that will be necessary to complete the work successfully.

Organize Resources

The project manager must organize the physical resources and the personnel allocated to the project so as to reach the objectives that have been defined. This involves choosing an office staff and setting up a chain of command, designing the number and kinds of positions that will be required, and assigning the duties and responsibilities of each.

Communicate

Communication is a key to the successful attainment of most of the other functions of the project manager. Not only does it keep the entire work force informed of problems and allow the manager to solicit solutions from them, it describes better methods, notifies of priorities, gives valuable feedback on jobs well done and prevents the kind of mix-ups that come only too often when one group of workers is not aware of what another group is doing even though group #1 depends on the function of group #2 for the successful completion of an assignment of their own. Without communication, the smallest glitch can turn into disaster.

Communication is also necessary to reconcile differing points of view that may arise on a project by individuals who have different ways of looking at the goals. (However, this is less likely to happen if a clear definition of goals and objectives and a thorough discussion among the different people on the project has taken place at the beginning.) In a data processing project, for example, systems users may push to get the system to perform a particular function as soon as possible, but the computing professionals insist that they need more time to perfect the system. If the project manager brings these two groups together for a face-to-face discussion and makes clear to them what the *needs of the project* are, the conflict can, in all probability, be resolved.

Keep Accurate Records

It is important to have a day by day record of the progression of the project, both to allow the project manager and the staff to spot trends that may, if not reversed, cause damage or delay, and to provide resource material from the experience that will be useful on a future project. This record keeping of all phases of the work is the responsibility, if not the direct task, of the project manager, and it is up to him or her to develop the most efficient and effective ways of getting complete picture of the project as it moves ahead. A later chapter will provide useful tools for this purpose.

Like a symphony orchestra, a stage or screen production, or any activity in which a number of people with overlapping and mutually dependent tasks aimed at achieving a single goal must work together, there must be one individual at the top providing the overall direction. In a business project, that individual, the person who provides authority and direction, is the project manager.

The above key responsibilities cover the first two of a project manager's three functions: *planning* and *organization*. How does the manager fulfill the third—*control* of the project? By setting up yardsticks to measure progress toward objectives, and to evaluate how effective the various activities within the project are. In the planning stage, standards are established. If these were general, they must be made specific so that managers can have a clear idea at all times of whether the standards are being met, or approached. Corrective measures are indicated whenever there is a deviation from the norms that have been established.

PHASES OF MANAGEMENT CONTROL

Management proceeds in phases in the control of a project. In the first phase, it is necessary to prevent deviations in the quality and quantity of resources used through a project. This means all the resources: financial, material, capital and human. In this first phase as well the manager enlists the participation and loyalty of the people working on the project.

In the second phase, the manager monitors actual ongoing operations to ensure that objectives, short-term and long-term, are being met. The guidelines below are helpful and will be discussed in detail later.

1. Have objectives been converted into meaningful standards?
2. Are performance standards reliable and accurate enough to assess the progress of a project?
3. Are reliable budgets and time schedules formulated so that an accurate comparison can be made between what was supposed to happen and what did happen?
4. Do means exist for a detailed comparison between resources expended as of a specific date and what was estimated for that particular date?
5. Does reevaluation occur whenever significant variances to project activities exist?

In the third phase, the manager concentrates on improving activities in those areas where it is apparent that the objectives are *not* being met, or are not likely to be met. This may involve rescheduling activities, reallocating resources, and altering the objectives.

In the next few sections of this book, a hypothetical construction firm's project management practices are described from the vantage point of its project manager. It would be extremely useful if you were to parallel this description with a project of your own—either an actual one that is being planned, or a hypothetical one. There is no need to have it be a construction project; rather, it should be one in your own area: finance, manufacturing, retailing, whatever—the principles and practices set forth here will be applicable to any kind of project. Take the suggestions, techniques, and forms and tailor them to your specific situation. You will then have a proven formula for successful project management.

Planning Page 1, the first form in Appendix B, is helpful in developing an overall viewpoint for a particular project. It's a good idea not only to use it yourself, but to make copies for others involved. A comparison of the individual completed copies can lead to a useful consensus.

2

A CASE STUDY IN PROJECT MANAGEMENT

The Northwest Construction Corporation (NCC) is a medium-sized firm that specializes in constructing small business complexes. Recently, it won a contract to build a two-story building for a real estate development firm known as Pacific Realty Associates.[*]

The firm wants the structure built on two acres of land in the Seattle, Washington, area. It will have a glass exterior and contain seventeen business offices and a cafeteria.

The roof will be equipped with patio facilities so leasees can entertain clients and friends. In addition, the building will have an outside parking facility with an electronic gate and a chainlink fence.

NCC SERVICES

The Northwest Construction Corporation provides several services to its clients. These services include:

[*] All the names in this case history are fictional.

- preparing a competitive bid or proposal for negotiation
- estimating costs and schedules from bid documents
- purchasing the services of contractors
- assembling a team of specialist subcontractors
- designing and creating the job site
- building the architect's office at the site
- setting up the job office and providing the superintendent with job clerks, layout engineers, and watchmen
- organizing activities at the construction site
- explaining and supporting the work for subcontractors
- coordinating subcontractor activity
- translating documents into task assignments for individuals
- interpreting documents for those doing the work
- supporting subcontractors with tools, equipment, and resources
- supporting its own workers with tools, equipment, and resources
- handling offsite activity relating to supply, fabrication, and preassembly required for the onsite work to be effective
- scheduling onsite work with offsite activity
- controlling the performance of the project participants
- facilitating cash flow from Pacific Realty Associates to NCC, suppliers, and contractors
- paying all bills and payrolls for its own and its subcontractors' work
- monitoring the progress of projects, especially in terms of time, cost and security
- overseeing the entire construction effort

SELECTING A PROJECT MANAGER

Richard Ronaldson has been assigned the position of project manager for this project. He has had previous experience in managing smaller projects. He was selected for other reasons as well.

Ronaldson is known for his ability to work well with a diverse group of people, from architects to laborers. He can direct people under negative circumstances as well as positive ones. Also, he has excellent organizational skills. He has the special ability to organize new efforts and to coordinate a multitude of activities. And perhaps most important, Ronaldson can communicate with virtually everyone, including technicians and nontechnicians.

In Appendix C, you will find a list headed *Characteristics and Capabilities of a Good Project Manager*. Use it to assess your own capabilities, and to know where your skills and abilities need strengthening.

After Christensen Associates, a prominent local architectural firm, had developed the appropriate architectural and structural diagrams and performed the necessary technical analysis for the projected building, NCC submitted a bid to Pacific Realty Association and was awarded the contract for the construction. Here is where Ronaldson's responsibilities as project manager begin.

THE PROJECT MANAGER AS PROJECT NEXUS

Ronaldson's first concern was to draw up an organizational chart that would ensure his central position, acting as link or clearing house between all the various major departments whose functions entered into the project, both on the staff/management/offsite side of the work and on the actual field side. He anticipated dealing with:

Staff/Management/Offsite	**Field/Line/Onsite**
Senior Management	Project Superintendent and
Estimating	his or her assistant
Sales	Field Engineers
Fiscal	Mechanical Engineers
Personnel	Field Accountants
Purchasing	Supervisors of the various
Equipment	work groups; some from
Pacific Realty, the owner	NCC, some from the sub-
Christensen Associates,	contractors
the architects' firm	

The chart Ronaldson drew up, showing the lines of communication between departments, all going directly or indirectly, through him is shown on pages 12–13.

List the various departments that will be involved, directly and indirectly, management/staff/offsite and field/line/onsite, on your own real or hypothetical project. Then draw a chart showing in a practical way how these various departments should be organized, with you, as project manager, as the core of communication. In doing so, carefully consider the significance of your interaction with each department, and what part input from it will play in the discharge of your particular responsibilities. The discussion below of Ronaldson's specific responsibilities can give you guidelines in assessing your own.

RONALDSON'S RESPONSIBILITIES

In some firms, the project manager and project superintendent are the same. At NCC, however, this is not the case. The project manager and superintendent have separate but interrelated responsibilities. Ronaldson has overall responsibility for the management of the project while Jeanne Haskins, the superintendent, is responsible for the actual running of the field office and directing operations at the site. She reports to Ronaldson on project activities.

At the inception of the project, Ronaldson's concern will be for staff responsibilities, because he partakes in planning and organizing. As the project moves into the implementation stage, his concern shifts toward line operations, since he must ensure that all activities proceed according to schedule.

Ronaldson seeks to maintain an especially strong liaison with the critical departments of Estimating, Fiscal, Purchasing, and Accounting. He knows that during the planning and implementation of the project, he must receive data from them to reevaluate cost and schedule criteria. His estimates and the monitoring of these estimates depend upon valid input from them.

Ronaldson also knows that he must maintain an effective liaison with his project superintendent. Haskins is directly

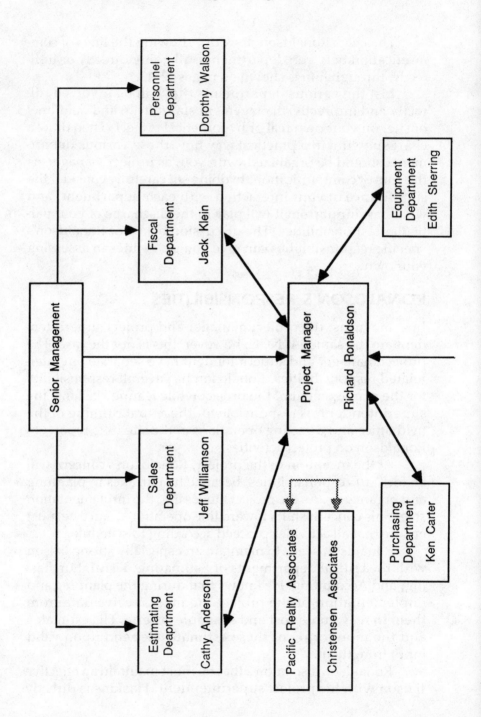

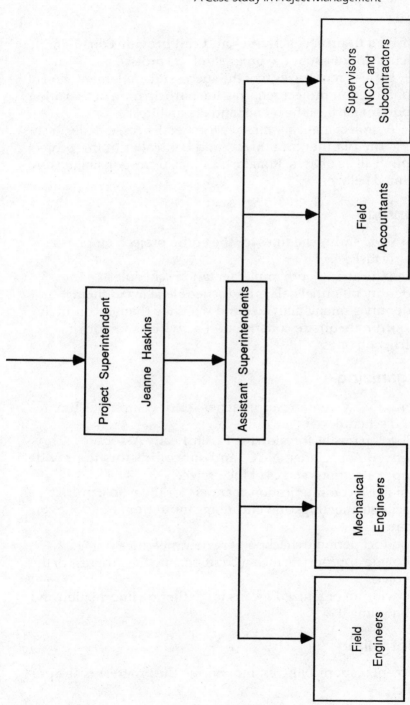

Figure 2-1 Organization Chart of NCC Project

involved in project activities and can provide considerable practical input about the progress of the project.

He also recognizes that the successful implementation of a construction project requires the participation of two other important parties: the owner and the architect.

A project manager must be a generalist; essentially, he or she is the planner, organizer, and controller of the project through all its phases. Ronaldson's specific responsibilities are outlined below.

Planning

- provide early schedules for the entire project, emphasizing early tasks
- prepare an in-depth implementation schedule
- identify potential delays and schedule to avoid them
- identify strategic activities and schedule them accordingly
- coordinate offsite construction activities with onsite construction ones

Organizing

- provide systematic approaches for developing estimates and schedules
- develop means for allowing Pacific Realty Associates, Christensen Associates, NCC, and subcontractors to provide input at various stages of the project
- establish communication channels for the whole project
- facilitate meetings and encourage input from everyone concerned
- conduct periodic checkpoint review meetings
- provide appropriate means for reporting the progress of the project
- provide an organized means for gathering information and compiling it

Controlling

- accept responsibility for monitoring the progress of the project

- update estimates at each major checkpoint
- ensure that each activity starts and finishes as planned
- conduct checkpoint review meetings with department heads to ascertain the exact details in each facet of the project
- publish daily construction reports which describe the activities that are occurring
- meet with Pacific Realty Associates and Christensen Associates to review the project's progress to ensure that the activities are producing what has been designed
- ensure that project progress information flows where it is needed
- compare project progress information with the master schedule
- analyze any variances that occur, especially between scheduled and actual completion dates
- document all changes to the schedule
- determine whether NCC has adequate personnel, equipment, and material to meet the schedule
- advise Pacific Realty Associates on the effect of any delays in meeting red-letter dates

While several of these responsibilities are specific to the project Ronaldson is managing, most are, or can easily be adapted to be, of a more general nature. Compare them with the list below, the responsibilities of the project manager of a data processing project for an insurance company (note that both this and Ronaldson's list are subdivided under the same three principal headings: Planning, Organizing and Controlling).

INSURANCE PROJECT: PROJECT MANAGER'S RESPONSIBILITIES

A project manager at an insurance company was responsible for planning, organizing, and controlling a data processing project. Here is a condensed list of these responsibilities.

Planning

- determine the major project phases of systems analysis,

systems design, systems development, systems implementation, and systems maintenance
- develop schedules to complete major project phases and activities
- devise a communications network to convey information and receive feedback
- develop time and cost estimates for each activity
- establish a reporting system on using resources

Organizing

- assess the required resources to complete each activity
- develop ways for project participants to provide input

Controlling

- monitor the progress of the project using various reports
- update resource estimates and schedules based upon input from project participants
- document all changes to resource allocations and schedules by maintaining logs and setting up project history files
- detect variances to plans pertaining to cost, resource allocations, and schedules
- review all requested changes to plans

Now draw up a list of your own responsibilities as manager of the project you have chosen. Use the two lists to give you guidelines; adapt them in the light of your knowledge of your own project.

The second worksheet in Appendix B, Planning Page 2, is an exercise in applying the principles outlined in this chapter to the project you have chosen. After filling it in, use it as a reference; if necessary, change it as experience dictates.

3

ESTABLISHING PROJECT DOCUMENTATION AND A COMMUNICATIONS NETWORK

A principal function of project managers is to coordinate activities and anticipate problems. To perform such tasks successfully, they must first establish a communications network to disseminate and to receive information.

Project managers should occupy a focal point in the corporate organization. They are the link between staff and line units. They are the ones who make sure that communication channels are functioning correctly.

AN EXAMPLE OF PROBLEM COMMUNICATIONS

The following example illustrates the importance of maintaining a communications network.

Pacific Realty Associates gave a steel manufacturer approval to develop steel beams according to specifications that were different from what was indicated in the original drawings. The applicable drawings were then updated. But neither NCC nor the subcontractor were informed of this change. They did not receive the revised drawings. The result, of course, was more than the delivery of misfitted steel beams.

In addition, serious delays occurred because NCC and the subcontractor had to recontact the manufacturer to have the "different" beams developed and delivered. The manufacturer insisted that the beams met the required specifications and showed the subcontractor the revised drawings. NCC and the subcontractor immediately complained to Pacific Realty Associates that it was not cooperating with them. Pacific Realty Associates insisted that it sent the drawings and blamed NCC and the subcontractor for not following instructions.

The result? Needless tension mounted among all three parties due to a breakdown in communications.

GOALS OF A COMMUNICATIONS NETWORK

There are two main goals in the establishment and maintenance of a communications network: disseminating information and obtaining feedback.

In a construction project, for example, architects and engineers need information from the owner to design the structure and develop diagrams. The owner requires information to secure financing for the project. Accountants and cost engineers must have sufficient information for their bookkeeping functions and payment of invoices. Manufacturers need appropriate specifications to produce material that meets the contractor's needs. The subcontractors require information to perform their specialized services effectively and efficiently.

The project manager has the responsibility to ensure that information is produced at the right time and delivered to the right place.

Feedback is also critical. It is especially important for the project manager, since he or she is responsible for the planning and control of the project. As a project manager, you'll need information for the creation and maintenance of schedules, particularly for some of the scheduling techniques, such as Gantt charts and Critical Path Method (CPM) diagrams that are discussed in a later chapter.

You'll also need feedback to spot delays that might occur, to judge whether they can be averted and whether they will have a serious effect, and to identify potential variances between estimated and probable completion dates. You'll want to have information that keeps you current on the progress of specific activities.

One of the most important reasons for getting continual feedback is so that it can be passed on to the people working on the project. All good managers know the importance of letting their subordinates know how they are doing if they want them to feel part of the team and function more productively.

How to do this—disseminate information, get feedback? Establish a communications network.

The Communications Network

What are the ingredients of a good communications network?

- an effective and relevant document for every instance where communication is necessary
- no unnecessary documents—almost every project participant hates unnecessary paperwork, and it should be kept to a minimum
- a system to ensure that the proper documents get to everyone who needs that particular information

How to accomplish this? Let's go to our case study and see how Ronaldson did it:

Ronaldson set up a matrix. Down the side he listed all the incoming documentation that could possibly be created in a project. Across the top he listed all the project participants. This is the tool he uses to set up his communication network; on it he will check off which documents go to which participants.

Note that there can be one matrix for incoming material and another for outgoing documents. The matrix is only meant as a guide, and there will be exceptions. Nevertheless, it serves as an effective means for distributing documents.

The matrix is the project manager's alone. Using it, the project manager is able to control the flow of documents, know who is getting what information, and keep abreast of project activities.

Ronaldson's matrix for his construction project is shown on pages 22–23. Using it as a guide, make one of your own for your hypothetical project. A number of the documents listed will be described in later chapters. You'll probably find that by changing a few labels on either axis of the chart, you can apply it to any project of your own. When the labels are in, check the squares showing who will get which documents.

DEVELOPING PROJECT MANUALS

The documentation distribution matrix is only one tool that you can employ. You should also develop and maintain a set of project manuals. Some manuals will be directed at a specific group of participants, while others will be pertinent to all.

For instance, subcontractors will have their own manual, while the superintendent will have another one. All manuals, whether specific or general in nature, should contain information on such items as you see in the following checklist. An overall project manual should be available that covers topics pertinent to everyone.

Project Manual Topics

- completion and distribution of forms
- approval processes
- standard routing and decision-making activities
- reporting instructions
- documentation handling
- activity completion measures
- position responsibilities
- report interpretation
- company organization
- project directory
- project overviews
- work flows
- project listing
- problem resolution

- scheduling and conducting meetings
- requesting resources
- purchasing procedures
- schedule changes
- contract interpretation
- equipment maintenance and repair
- transportation requests
- employment practices and records
- safety procedures and practices
- field administration
- responses to scheduling and resource allocation variances

Each manual should contain information in the form of a procedure or a work flow or both. Work flows are particularly effective in displaying information in graphic form. As an example, take a proposal for a change in specifications. Here is how a change order proposal (which is a request for issuing a change order to alter project specifications) is handled at NCC:

1. A subcontractor obtains a blank change order proposal form, completes it, and forwards it to the project superintendent. She reviews the information and sends it to Richard Ronaldson.
2. After reviewing the information, Ronaldson signs it, photocopies it to store in the project history file (explained later), and determines whether there are others who should see it. For instance, does he need to contact the *architect* at Christensen Associates? If he does, he must get the architect's approval and then determine if there are any significant changes that need the *owner's* review and approval. In that case, he contacts Pacific Realty for their consideration of the proposal.
3. Ultimately, Ronaldson must approve or disapprove the proposal and notify the superintendent.

Figure 3-2 is a workflow showing how a change order is handled on the NCC project. In Appendix C, there is a sample of a change order proposal form.

Participants

	CPM Diagram	Design Documents	Daily Equipment Reports	Inspection Reports	Daily Material Records	Purchase Orders
Subcontractor	×					
Field Accountants	×					
Assistant Superintendent	×					
Mechanical Engineers	×					
Field Engineer	×					
Superintendent	×					
Equipment	×					
Purchasing	×					
Personnel	×					
Fiscal	×					
Sales	×					
Estimating	×					
Arch-Engineer	×					
Owner	×					
Project Manager	×	×	×	×	×	×

Documentation

Other Correspondence	X										
Photographs	X										
Labor Requirements Chart	X										
Minutes of Meetings	X										
Daily Time Report	X										
Change Orders	X										
Status Reports	X										
Daily Construction Report	X										
Contracts	X										
Activity Status Reports	X										

Figure 3-1 Documentation Distribution Matrix

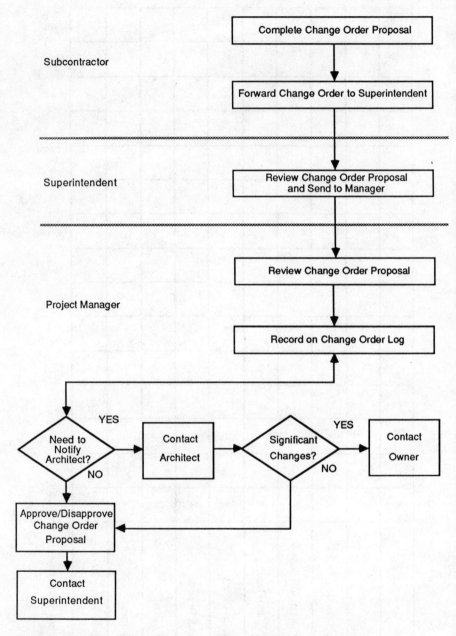

Figure 3-2 Sample of Work Flow on Handling Change Order Proposals

CREATING A PROJECT HISTORY FILE

The project history file, sometimes referred to as a project notebook, is a collection of documents on the planning, organizing, and controlling of the project. The file is valuable as a:

- repository of information on the current status of the project
- diary of the life of the project
- record on the amount of time, resources, and staff devoted to the project
- storage medium for future research and analysis on this project and future ones

To be fully effective, a project history file must not only contain the correct documentation—everything relevant to the history of the project and to any future use to which it may be put. It must also be organized in such a way that the documentation can most easily be used. While there are numerous different kinds of divisions that could be made, we believe that the project manager in our case study, Richard Ronaldson, has hit upon the simplest and best by subdividing his project history into the three basic sections we've already set up as the three phases of the project:

- planning
- organizing
- controlling

and adding one *more* to them for miscellaneous documents.

Appendix C contains a detailed outline showing the sections and subdivisions of the NCC project history file. In making up your own, include the documents under each main heading that you find relevant to your own project. (Note that some of the subheadings listed on the example deal with documents that have not been discussed yet; they will be dealt with in future sections of this work.)

OTHER COMMUNICATION TOOLS

Communicating among the participants in a project by distribution of documents is practical and valuable. It's a good way to handle the day to day flow of information, and having it written down avoids misunderstandings and provides a record.

However, there are occasions when something more is called for, when it is necessary to have discussions, exchange viewpoints, or resolve differences that may have arisen. The obvious answer is: Call a meeting.

It's necessary to give serious thought in the planning stage to the question of meetings. They can be overdone. Time better spent on the job can be frittered away in superfluous meetings. On the other hand, a productive meeting when it is really necessary is a positive factor in morale and efficiency, and has the added virtue of reinforcing the participants' feeling that they are being consulted as part of the team.

Here is how Richard Ronaldson approaches the subject of meetings:

First, he has set up a system of scheduled checkpoint review meetings, which he holds at the beginning and end of each phase of the project. Each participant discusses the details of the completed phase and the forthcoming one. In addition, they discuss variances between planned and actual performance.

In addition, he holds meetings that are not regularly scheduled, but called whenever he feels one is really necessary. He may call a meeting when a significant change is required in the drawings or specifications, or when changes occur that are extremely sensitive to the owner or the architect-engineer. At these meetings, all the parties have a chance to exchange views and communicate their needs.

He might call a meeting when ambiguities crop up over project objectives, or to resolve sharp disagreements over how a job should be done or who should do it. This kind of disagreement should be infrequent if lines of authority and responsibility are clearly drawn from the first.

The project manager should go into the meeting with a clear agenda in mind, and a definite idea about how to conduct it to avoid time-wasting repetition or distraction from the purpose at hand.

Ronaldson conducts a meeting efficiently by first describing the nature of the problem that has inspired the meeting. He then leads a discussion from all those present, letting everyone freely express his or her ideas, but keeping the discussion firmly to the point. He makes certain that all the salient points pertinent to the subject are brought up and discussed, and if a decision is necessary, brings the discussion to a close with a call for one to be reached.

At all meetings, Ronaldson has minutes taken, which are distributed to all the participants and included in the project history file.

When meetings are not practical—as when a project is widespread geographically—it is sometimes necessary to fall back on less efficient means of communication. Depending on the urgency of the subject, and whether give-and-take is desirable, the telephone (preferably with a leased line, if there is much long-distance calling) and the mail will have to do.

Planning Page 3, in Appendix B, will help you pull together some of the suggestions discussed in this chapter.

4

THE GANTT CHART FOR EARLY-STAGE PROJECT SCHEDULING

Naturally, anyone in charge of an ongoing project will work out a schedule for it. But the ideal schedule is one that provides an effective means for planning, organizing and controlling a project. It should let the project manager quickly anticipate financial, material, and personnel requirements, and analyze the effects of temporary delays and suspensions caused by any number of problems, such as labor shortages, funding difficulties, poor subcontractor coordination, late arrival of diagrams, or defective workmanship.

The most effective kind of schedule, therefore, is a graphic display. To make such a display, it is useful to start out with a Gantt or bar chart, which is extremely helpful in the early phases of the project. As the project progresses and as activities become more complex and detailed, the Gantt chart has certain limitations that make it desirable to switch to some other scheduling tool, and we have found that a network diagram, either of the PERT (Program Evaluation and Review Technique) or the CPM (Critical Path Method) serve the purpose well.

CONSTRUCTING THE GANTT CHART

The general procedure is to break the overall project down into its separate but interrelated subprojects. List each phase, each effort that produces some specific result. Looking at the whole project, and "exploding" or subdividing it into discrete, manageable units is called Project Breakdown Structuring (PBS). For the Gantt chart, it is necessary to break the project down only to the phase level.

When the list of subprojects is complete and in proper sequential order, each having a specific and verifiable character and a specific time of completion, estimate the duration of each phase and decide which can be carried out concurrently — you'll find that some can while others must wait upon the completion of the previous phases.

Preliminary Steps in Constructing a Gantt Chart for the NCC project

1. Ronaldson broke the overall project down into separate phases:

   - sitework
   - excavation
   - foundation work
   - structural work
   - concrete work
   - flooring
   - roofing
   - masonry
   - finishing
   - internal work

2. He then estimated the duration in weeks of each phase:

   - sitework   2 weeks
   - excavation   3
   - foundation work   7

- structural work   10
- concrete work   8
- flooring   5
- roofing   6
- masonry   5
- finishing   8
- internal work   34

With this information, it is possible to construct the Gantt diagram.

First, let's consider a similar list; the breakdown made and the time estimated for a typical data processing project. This should demonstrate that the process is applicable to any sort of project.

Phase Breakdown and Duration Estimate for a Data Processing Project:

- Investigation and analysis 4 weeks
- Output design   8
- Input design   6
- Systems file design   5
- Systems control design   8
- Design approval   3
- Programming   7
- Testing   6
- Implementation   3
- Evaluation   7

It is just as possible to construct a Gantt chart from the above data as it is from Ronaldson's breakdown. Draw up a list of subprojects for your own project, and estimate the duration of each, so that you can go on with the description of the procedure of constructing a Gantt chart.

1. Draw a horizontal line for your X-axis. This represents the time scale for completing the project, and should be divided into as many equal sections as you need *months* for your overall schedule.
2. Perpendicular to this, and at the left, construct the Y-axis,

and list, sequentially, the phases of the project, equidistant from one another.

3. Under each solid bar, and contiguous to it, draw a hollow bar that can be used to show, as the project progresses, the extent to which a phase has been completed. Slanted lines can be drawn within these open bars to show what percent of each phase has been completed at any time.

The Gantt chart Ronaldson has drawn up to represent the scheduling of his construction project is shown on the following page.

After constructing the chart, Ronaldson has at his disposal a graphic display of the starting date, completion date, and duration of each phase as well as of the whole project. This is a tool that is needed by virtually all the major participants in a project. Specifically for the NCC construction project, the following people and organizations make use of it.

Christensen Associates needs the bar chart since it originally designed the structure. It needs to know the approximate time for each phase so that it can, in advance, design, modify, or replace diagrams that are used by NCC. Also, it needs to know when the diagrams are needed so that it can provide itself enough lead time to prepare the documents.

The subcontractors (those participants who apply a special knowledge to a particular section of work) need a tentative schedule so that they can predict their responsibilities for completing future activities.

Certain manufacturers need it so they can prepare the material in advance and deliver it prior to its installation. This is particularly important for those items that require a long lead time, such as steel, which takes several months to obtain. The Gantt chart provides the manufacturer with a gauge to judge when to manufacture and deliver the material.

The superintendent, Jeanne Haskins, needs to know what major activities will occur and when. Periodically, she uses the chart to ascertain when to contact other participants involved in the project, such as Ken Carter (the manager of the purchasing department), who is responsible for ordering material for the project.

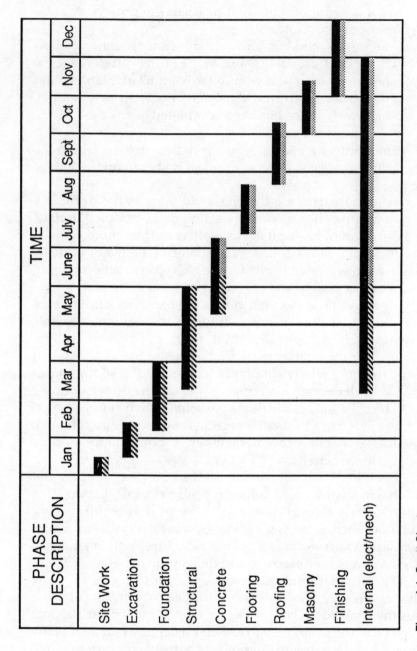

Figure 4-1 Gantt Chart

Cathy Anderson of the estimating department needs the Gantt chart to prepare detailed estimates on the costs of the project. The figures can then be submitted to the purchasing department to be included in the bidding.

The purchasing department needs the chart to determine material requirements and to provide dates for the bidding process. Carter, or a member of his staff, can then invite bids.

The fiscal department, under Jack Klein, requires the document to provide a projection of cash flow requirements throughout the course of the project. The cash comes from Pacific Realty Associates to pay for contract work and to purchase materials.

Edith Sherring, of the equipment department, requires a Gantt chart for coordinating the use, maintenance, and purchase of equipment during the different phases of the project.

Pacific Realty Associates has a vested interest in the project, and needs to know the timetable for its progress so as to ensure that its eventual completion date will be reached.

Finally, the field supervisors and engineers responsible for the actual implementation of the project must have the bar chart to ascertain when their activities are to begin and end.

LIMITATIONS OF GANTT CHARTS

During the early stages of a project, the Gantt chart serves as a means for putting a perspective on the project. But as the project moves forward and as activities become more complex and detailed, the limitations of scheduling this way become apparent.

One problem is that such charts do not reflect the various relationships or dependencies existing among phases. Although it doesn't take an expert to realize that the laying of foundations is dependent upon the excavation of the area, there are other, more technical relationships that only someone with extensive construction experience would recognize.

Gantt charts also do not show the effect of a delay in a phase. They do not indicate the existence of a network of activities. A delay in one set of activities will inevitably cause an eventual delay in starting future activities. In the Gantt chart, this consequence is often difficult to detect. Instead, in many cases, the reader might easily assume the two activities are separable and have no effect on one another.

Also, a Gantt chart does not show the results of either a hypothetical early or late start on project phases. It affords little predictive or analytical value. The reader of the chart will find it exceedingly difficult to adjust the scale whenever an early or late start is anticipated, since he or she will not know of the existing dependencies.

Nor does the Gantt chart indicate the percentage of total work that each phase represents. And it does not show which phases are critical to the completion of the project within an allotted time.

Ultimately, the Gantt chart does not reflect the revisions in planning activities. It does not effectively indicate the effect of delays in the scheduling of activities. When a delay does occur, the effect is recorded after the fact, which is too late for corrective action.

As you can see, these problems are inherent to the nature of the chart, and not simply some that arise on a construction project such as NCC's. Look at the list drawn up on page 30 for preparing a Gantt chart for a data processing project. Obviously, it's not possible to tell if a dependency exists between output design and systems control design. Nor could you tell what the impact on the project would be if a phase like input design occurs three weeks later.

During the early stages of a project, the Gantt chart serves as an excellent communications tool for the project manager and provides a basis for doing preliminary resource and financial estimates. As a project progresses, however, the project manager needs a more refined and effective tool for scheduling. The tool is the Critical Path Method (CPM).

Before we begin a discussion of network diagrams, take a few minutes to review the list you have made for your own Gantt charts. Note your general comments on Planning Page 4 in Appendix B for future reference on specific projects.

5

CONSTRUCTING NETWORK DIAGRAMS

After you've made use of a Gantt chart and are ready for a more refined planning tool, one that is more sophisticated and definitive, you will turn to the network diagram.

WHAT IS A NETWORK DIAGRAM?

A network diagram is a graphic representation of a series of activities and events depicting the various aspects of a project and the order in which these activities and events must occur. It reflects all activities and events from the beginning to the ending of the project.

An activity is the work or effort needed to complete a particular event which uses time and other resources and has a definable beginning and ending.

An event is an accomplishment at a specific point in time and uses no resources. Further, activities ending in an event must be completed before any activity starting from that event can begin.

A network diagram is used whenever several activities and events are combined.

35

ADVANTAGES OF NETWORK DIAGRAMS

Network diagrams help you to:

- present a graphic depiction of the interdependencies of activities
- estimate accurately the requirements for resources, such as personnel, equipment, and materials
- determine costs associated with scheduled activities
- plan and schedule in detail *before* the beginning of a project
- provide a convenient means to communicate and document project plans, schedules, and other information
- consider the effect of time and resource constraints on an activity or project
- predict project duration
- determine the shortest duration of a project
- determine and eliminate unnecessary activities
- concentrate on critical activities
- ensure that all participants comply with time schedules
- detect variances from schedules and deal with the effects of those variances
- revise existing schedules whenever a potential problem occurs
- examine alternative methods for carrying out a project under varying time and resource requirements
- transfer excess resources assigned to some activities to others needing more resources

PERT VS. CPM

You have the option to choose between two types of network diagrams. The first is PERT; the second is CPM.

PERT   In 1958, the United States Navy needed a way to monitor and control the Polaris missile program. It especially needed a method for minimizing the conflicts, delays, and interruptions that so frequently plague government projects. To accomplish that, the Navy developed the *Program Evaluation and Review Technique* (PERT).

The Navy discovered that PERT enabled it to determine time schedules and resource requirements for each activity. It found that PERT facilitated the rescheduling and reassignment of resources with a minimum delay to projects. Furthermore, it saw that PERT helped Navy personnel to work with contractors by providing a graphic means for showing the negative effects of delays on a project.

CPM   Around the same time that the Navy built its Polaris missiles using PERT, a civilian company developed its own kind of network diagram. E.I. du Pont de Nemours, the huge chemical company, sought to devise a way to determine accurate time and cost estimates for the construction of several chemical plants. They needed a system that would tell them whether work was falling behind schedule at any given time and whether to take action to bring the work back on schedule. Between 1956 and 1958, it developed the famous Critical Path Method (CPM).

Viewing the Differences

Some distinct differences exist between PERT and CPM. PERT uses three time estimates per activity while CPM requires only one. For PERT diagrams, the times are:

Optimistic time (a)—the time the firm can complete an activity or project under the most ideal conditions.
Most likely time (m)—the most realistic time estimate for completing an activity or project under normal conditions.
Pessimistic time (b)—the time the firm can complete an activity or project under the worst conditions.

Once the three times are determined, the Expected Time (te) is calculated for each activity. The formula for this calculation is:

$$te = \frac{a + 4m + b}{6}$$

As an example, let us see how Ronaldson would calculate the expected time for excavating the site of his construction project by a digger. After careful consideration, he determines the following times:

Optimistic Time (a) = 3 days
Most Likely Time (m) = 5 days
Pessimistic Time (b) = 8 days

He would then perform the calculation:

$$\text{te} = \frac{3 + 4(5) + 8}{6}$$

$$= \frac{3 + 20 + 8}{6}$$

$$= \frac{31}{6}$$

$$= 5.1 \text{ days}$$

Following the PERT formula, Ronaldson would thus allow or anticipate 5.1 days to excavate the site by digger.

PERT diagrams also require an emphasis on the accomplishment of events, or milestones. Time, not milestones, is critical to projects using CPM diagrams. Not surprisingly, CPM relies upon a single estimate, unlike PERT.

Projects using PERT usually face fewer constraints than projects using CPM. PERT is often used in government projects, especially research and development ones, like those related to the space program, military defense, and medical research.

In each of these projects, the achievement of a specific result—the successful test firing of an air defense missile or the production of a reliable lunar lander—is more important than completing a project within a specified budget or period of time.

CPM is more applicable to construction projects. It works best when time can be estimated accurately and costs can be determined in advance. Construction projects continually face budget constraints and restrictive completion dates. Operating within the constraints is important; otherwise, the contractor may be plagued with legal problems and penalties.

Preparatory to constructing the diagram, it is necessary to get as much information from as many individuals as possible, particularly from the key people on the project. In this way, the network will be of the greatest relevance and best meet the needs of the participants—therefore, it will be of the greatest use to the project and the project manager.

APPROACHES TO GATHERING INPUT FOR THE NETWORK

There are four possible approaches for the project manager to get the necessary data for the network:

Democratic

This would gather together as many key individuals as possible in a physical meeting. At the meeting, all the participants would discuss the entire project, and would make commitments in the process. After the meeting, the project manager has only to refine the diagram.

While this approach allows everyone to participate, and reinforces the feeling of individuals that they are an integral and important part of the project, it is time consuming and difficult to implement. There is much danger of the meeting getting bogged down in disagreements on commitment, sequences and activities.

Consultant

This involves calling in an outside consultant to talk the project through with a limited number of key members of the project, and then prepare the diagram. This method, while having the advantage of an objective view of the project, is again time-consuming, and would be expensive.

Leader

Here the project manager goes it alone. Receiving input only on an informal basis, he or she notes all the significant activities and events without help from other participants in the project. It would fall on the project manager to determine the significant commitment dates and the sequential flow of the diagram.

This approach is a burden on the project manager. It also presupposes that that individual has all the knowledge to construct an accurate and objective diagram. Without the participation of at least some of the project participants, there is liable to be resentment among the personnel, and a reluctance to accept the leader's diagram.

Oligarchic

Here the project manager invites only a limited number of key people to help draw the diagram. They would participate in the same way those in the democratic approach would do, but since there are fewer people involved, the process would be far more manageable. Again, after it was over, it would fall to the project manager to refine the diagram that had been drawn up.

Project manager Richard Ronaldson chooses the oligarchic approach, and invites only key decision-makers to take part. He schedules their meeting far enough in advance to ensure that everyone has the opportunity to prepare questions, remarks and other concerns. Two to three weeks should be sufficient time, if all the participants are told at the outset what will be required of the meeting.

At the meeting, here is the agenda that Ronaldson has drawn up. This is what the people attending must decide:

- What are the major activities of the project?
- What are the major events of the project?

- What is the finish date of each activity?
- Whose responsibility is each activity?
- What are the general resource requirements of each activity?
- What is the sequence of activities and events?

CONDUCTING A NETWORK MEETING

Ronaldson schedules his meeting in a conference room equipped with a large circular table and a big blackboard. When the meeting begins, he makes sure that everyone is present and that a secretary is taking notes.

He opens the meeting by announcing its objectives and what exactly he expects from everyone. He also announces the constraints and requirements imposed upon the project, as well as explaining that the Gantt chart developed earlier serves as a basis for discussion.

The participants in such a meeting will break down each major phase listed in the Gantt chart into activities. This process is known as Work Breakdown Structuring (WBS) and is based on the same principles as Project Breakdown Structuring, which was covered in the previous chapter.

WBS enables everyone to list those activities necessary for completing a project phase. It requires participants to think logically about how to complete a phase. It provides for detailed planning, allowing for better control. It improves the ability of the contractor's staff to define costs and budgets. It facilitates tracking the progress of a project, because definable benchmarks are established. It links together the major activities and events in an orchestrated way. And it maintains accountability throughout the project because a definable, clear activity is assigned to someone or some unit.

As the meeting determines activities, the participants select those that have a definable beginning and ending and are clearly conceptualized. These activities, in turn, should lead to certain milestones, or events. Each activity should have a uniqueness and should possess discrete, scheduled start and completion points. In addition, each activity must be measurable in either dollars, hours, or some other concrete units of measure.

While breaking each phase into activities, these are questions to keep in mind:

- What activities must be performed?
- Which activities have a higher priority?
- Why does each activity have to be completed?
- What amount of resources (money, equipment, manpower, time, etc.) is required for each activity?
- What amount of resources is available for each activity?
- Who will perform the activity?
- Where will the activity be performed?
- How will the activity be performed?

CREATING THE ROUGH DIAGRAM

As each activity is defined, the project manager draws a preliminary version of the network diagram on a large sheet of paper spread out on the conference table, noting the activity, the resulting event, the completion date, its logical position in the sequence, and any other pertinent factors. The secretary should record the responses to each question.

To collect the necessary diagram data, the project manager can use an activity description form like the one in Figure 5-1 to record information on project activities. The form makes it possible to record the sequence number, description, duration, starting point, and ending point.

At this point, two questions often plague designers of network diagrams.

- How many events should the network have?
- How detailed should the breakdown be?

The answers to these two questions are subjective. The number of activities and events and the level of detail depend on the complexity of the project and your own background in CPM analysis. For the NCC project, for example—and for most other projects as well—it is satisfactory to break the work down to a tertiary level.

For example, the NCC project has three definable levels: the entire project, the different phases, and the activities re-

| Activity | | Duration (Days) | Event | |
Sequence No.	Description		From starting event (i)	To completion event (j)
1	Clear Site	2	1	2
2	Conduct Survey	2	2	3
3	Rough Grade	1	3	4
4	Transport Tools to Site	1	4	7
5	Prepare Access Road	1	1	5
6	Transport Huts to Site	1	5	6
7	Prepare Concrete Mixing Area	1	6	7
8	Transport Crane to Site	1	7	8
9	Assemble Crane	2	8	9
10	Excavate for Sewer	2	9	10

Figure 5-1 An Activity Description Form for the NCC Construction Project

quired to accomplish each phase. Seldom is it necessary to divide a project down to the task or subtask level. That usually results in over-planning, over-organizing, and over-controlling.

The project manager now draws a skeletal diagram using the same symbols that she or he will use to refine it for the finished version. These symbols are simply a conventional "shorthand" that everyone involved can recognize and thus understand the diagram. The project manager records all the events and activities, using symbols that typically signify these aspects. As shown below, an event is represented by a circle, identified with a unique number. An activity is bounded by two events and is represented by an arrow.

Under most circumstances, a succeeding event is also a preceding one. As the succeeding event, it represents the completion of an activity, and is designated by the letter j. In its character of starting event for an activity, it is designated by the letter i.

Figure 5-1 is an activity description table for the NCC construction project. In it, Event #2 is the succeeding event for

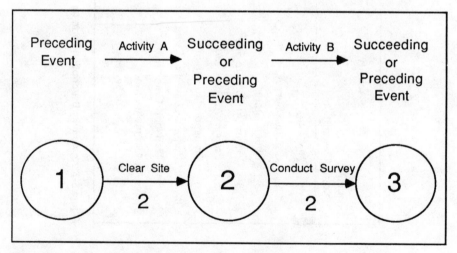

Figure 5-2 Form for Preceding and/or Succeeding Events

Activity A, but also the preceding event for Activity B. This basic principle is followed through the entire process of creating the diagram. All preceding activities must be completed before any succeeding ones can occur. Thus, Activity B cannot occur until Activity A is performed.

The preliminary document is more than a sequence of activities for the project. It is also an agreement between the different participants. All have expressed their concerns and commitments at the meeting and have had them reflected in the diagram.

Once the meeting is over, and the preliminary diagram made, the project manager has the crucial task of constructing an accurate, sophisticated network diagram. The project manager will do this without altering the basic structure of the diagram, using the Gantt chart, the activity description form, the minutes of the meeting, his or her own knowledge, and the preliminary CPM diagram as tools.

Keep in mind, however, that the accepted general framework for the network is not the final course. If better ideas arise during the project, the project manager must be willing to reflect them in the network and to distribute those changes. Constructing the network is an ongoing process. If conditions change and the network does not incorporate them, the diagram will have little relevance.

Take a minute here to think about your own best approach to network diagram input. Look over the following six steps. Developing your own responses should give you a good idea of what will work best for you.

1. Determine the information you need to have.
2. Decide what information you can obtain yourself.
3. Decide what information you will need from someone else.
4. Determine who needs to provide input.
5. Determine who wants to provide input.
6. If a meeting is held, determine who will be able to attend it at the scheduled time and place.

6

LAYING THE GROUNDWORK FOR USING THE CRITICAL PATH METHOD

In refining your own network diagram, follow the fundamental guidelines that make up this list. If you're instructing other project managers, make copies of the list and see that they understand the guidelines.

GUIDELINES FOR CONSTRUCTING A NETWORK DIAGRAM

1. Bound each activity with a starting and ending event, or node.
2. Use only one arrow between any two events.
3. Have one starting and finishing event for the entire network.
4. Organize activities into a logical and natural sequence.
5. Assign a duration to each activity (duration is the estimated time spent on an activity).
6. Construct a diagram that flows left-to-right and top-down.
7. Assign a unique number for each node, or event, on the diagram (a node signifies a point when all preceding ac-

tivities are complete and all succeeding activities are commencing).

8. Recognize that the occurrence of an activity falls under one of three circumstances:

   (a) an activity may precede other activities
   (b) an activity may follow another activity
   (c) an activity may occur simultaneously with another activity

ASSIGNING I-J DESIGNATIONS

When constructing the final version of the diagram, assign an i-j designation for each activity, a combination of the beginning node and ending node of an activity. (Note that the i-j designations for each phase of the NCC project were shown in Figure 5-1 in the two right-hand columns).

Each i-j designation indicates the beginning and ending node for each activity reflected in the network diagram. The i-j designation is unique to that activity; that is, no other activity has the same i-j designation. And the number at the tail of the arrow is lower than the number at the head of the arrow.

The i-j designations are assigned after the diagram has been completely drawn. This facilitates the drawing of the diagram by making it easier for you to add activities you may have missed. Otherwise, you will have to reassign i-j designations to activities, especially if you must resequence those activities.

When assigning numbers to each of the nodes in a diagram, you have two paths to follow. You can use either vertical numbering or horizontal numbering. Vertical numbering requires reading the diagram from two perspectives; top-down, left-to-right. This way is difficult for most people, since they usually read left-to-right only, and not top-down and left-to-right at the same time.

Horizontal numbering, however, makes it easier to read and understand a diagram because people are primarily accustomed to reading left-to-right and perceive charts from a horizontal perspective. See Figure 6-1 for examples of these two numbering schemes.

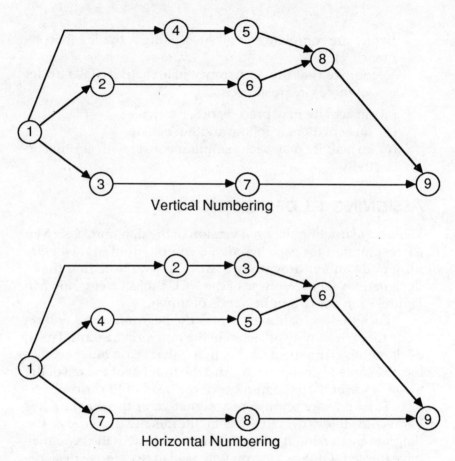

Figure 6-1 Vertical and Horizontal Numbering

FILLING OUT THE DIAGRAM

Along with numbering the events, record a brief description of each activity above the arrow, as shown in Figure 6-2. The description usually begins with an active verb like "install" or "complete" and an object, normally a noun. The main point is to be brief but descriptive so that someone with little prior knowledge can read and understand the diagram.

On the lower horizontal part of each arrow, indicate the duration of the activity in numeric form.

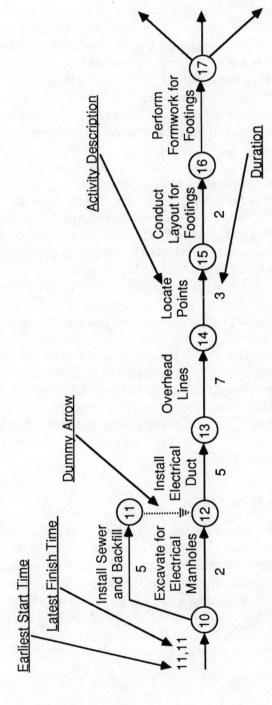

Figure 6-2 Miscellaneous Items Displayed in a Partial Network Diagram

- The length of the arrow is insignificant. One arrow longer than another does not mean that it is more important than the other or that it has a longer duration.
- Crossovers of arrows should be avoided whenever possible. Occasionally an arrow leading from one event to another crosses over another arrow. This is acceptable when it is unavoidable, but too many crossovers make a network diagram confusing.
- No event should be without a unique number and no activity should be without an i-j designation.
- Some activities cannot be shown by a solid arrow; instead, a dashed line is used. This dashed line symbolizes a dummy arrow and indicates an activity that uses no resources or time. (See the arrow between 11 and 12 in Figure 6-2.) It is used best to indicate that the failure to complete an activity hinders the start of two or more activities between two nodes.
- Scheduling certain activities to take place at the same time, concurrent scheduling, is an excellent way to reduce the overall time to complete a project and allows for greater flexibility in scheduling. With concurrent scheduling, some activities can be moved ahead or held back without delaying the entire schedule. In this example, it refers to an activity that is not directly related to the project activities, but whose failure to complete will hinder completion of one or more subsequent activities.

PREPARING A SCHEDULE

Determining the schedule of a project, and the critical path, is, after all, the purpose of having drawn a network diagram. Establishing time estimates enables the project manager to determine the beginning and ending dates for each activity, which requires developing an activity time chart. As an example, let's look at the one Ronaldson created for his construction project.

In constructing your own activity time chart:

- list all activities according to ascending i-designation
- record a short description of each activity
- indicate the duration of each activity
- compute and record such critical times as

  - earliest start
  - earliest finish
  - latest start
  - latest finish
  - free float
  - total float

Calculating Activity Times

Activity times provide you with the data necessary to determine resource requirements and to measure the progress of a schedule.

Earliest Start.   The earliest an activity can begin if all activities before it are finished is called the Earliest Start. It is the earliest time that an activity leaves its i-mode.

To calculate the Earliest Start for an activity, we use the Forward Pass Method (FPM). The FPM helps to determine the earliest possible start and finish times per activity by looking at the network diagram. To make these determinations, we make two assumptions:

- that the project begins at time zero, and
- that each activity begins immediately after the conclusion of the preceding activity.

Using the diagram in Figure 6-4 as an example, and reading it from left-to-right, Ronaldson has recorded above each node the Earliest Start time for that activity. Thus, the Earliest Start time for "Rough Grade" is 4 days (0 days + 2 days + 2 days). He records that time on the activity time chart in Figure 6-3. He then uses these sums to calculate the Earliest Finish times.

i-j	Description	Duration (days)	Earliest Start	Earliest Finish	Latest Start	Latest Finish	Floats Free	Floats Total
1-2	Clear Site	2	0	2	0	2	0	0
1-5	Prepare Access to Roads	1	0	1	3	4	0	3
2-3	Conduct Survey	2	2	4	2	4	0	0
3-4	Rough Grade	1	4	5	4	5	0	0
4-7	Transport Tools to Site	1	5	6	5	6	0	0
5-6	Transport Huts to Site	1	1	2	4	5	0	3
6-7	Prepare Concrete Mixing Area	1	2	3	5	6	0	3
7-8	Transport Crane to Site	1	6	7	6	7	0	0
8-9	Assemble Crane	2	7	9	7	9	0	0
9-10	Excavate for Sewer	2	9	11	9	11	0	0

Figure 6-3 Activity Time Chart

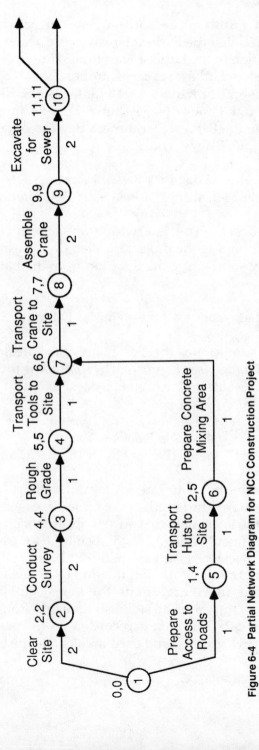

Figure 6-4 Partial Network Diagram for NCC Construction Project

Earliest Finish. The earliest time an activity can be completed is called the Earliest Finish. It is calculated by adding the duration to the Earliest Start time. Thus,
Earliest Finish = Earliest Start + Duration

Ronaldson, for instance, calculates the Earliest Finish time for "Rough Grade" (see Figure 6-3) by adding the duration, 1 day, to the Earliest Start time, 4 days, to obtain the Earliest Finish time, 5 days. Thus,

$$5 \text{ days} = 1 \text{ day} + 4 \text{ days}$$
$$(\text{Earliest Finish}) = (\text{Earliest Start}) + (\text{Duration})$$

Latest Start. The latest time an activity can begin without lengthening the project is called the Latest Start. It is calculated by subtracting the duration from the Latest Finish time. Thus,

$$\text{Latest Start} = \text{Latest Finish - Duration}$$

Ronaldson, for instance, calculates the Latest Start time for "Rough Grade" (see Figure 6-3) by *subtracting* the duration, 1 day, from the Latest Finish time, 5 days, to obtain the Latest Start time. Thus,

$$4 \text{ days} = 5 \text{ days} - 1 \text{ day}$$
$$(\text{Latest Start Time}) = (\text{Latest Finish Time}) - (\text{Duration})$$

Latest Finish. The latest time an activity can finish without extending the length of the project is called the Latest Finish. It is the latest time that an activity enters its j-mode.

You can calculate the Latest Finish time for each activity by using the Backward Pass Method (BPM).

Reading the network diagram in Figure 6-4 from right-to-left, record above each node the Latest Finish time for each activity. Thus, the Latest Finish time for "Rough Grade" is 5 days (11-2-2-1-1). That is recorded on the activity time chart shown in Figure 6-3 and used to calculate the Latest Start time.

Calculating the Float

Once the Earliest Start, Earliest Finish, Latest Start, and Latest Finish times have been calculated for each activity, calculate the Free Float and Total Float times.

Float time is essentially the time flexibility allowed in the scheduling of activities; that is, it is the amount of surplus time available to complete an activity. You must ensure that each activity is completed within the Earliest Start time and the Latest Finish time. Whenever the difference between the Earliest Start time and the Latest Finish time exceeds the duration for any particular activity, that excess time is called float.

Two basic types of float exist: Free Float and Total Float.

Free Float.   This float represents the amount of time that an activity can be delayed without affecting the float of succeeding activities. The amount of Free Float available is dependent upon the amount of Free Float shared with any preceding activities.

You calculate the Free Float for each activity by subtracting the duration and Earliest Start time from the Earliest Finish time. Thus,

Free Float = Earliest Finish Time - Earliest Start Time -Duration

For example, Ronaldson calculates the Free Float for "Preparing Access to Roads" by performing the following calculations:

$$0 \text{ days} = 1 \text{ day} - 0 \text{ days} - 1 \text{ day}$$
$$(\text{Free Float}) = (\text{Earliest Finish}) - (\text{Earliest Start}) - (\text{Duration})$$

According to Figure 6-3, none of the activities has Free Float. Ronaldson realizes this means that none of the activities can be delayed without affecting the total float on succeeding activities.

Total Float.   The other float you must calculate is the Total Float. It provides the total amount of flexibility in scheduling activities on a non-critical path, or the time an ac-

	Description	Duration (days)	Earliest		Latest		Floats	
			Start	Finish	Start	Finish	Free	Total
1-2	Design Interface	2	0	2	0	2	0	0
1-3	Conduct Walk-through	1	0	1	1	2	0	1
2-4	Modify Programs	5	2	7	2	7	0	0
4-5	Run Tests	2	7	9	7	9	0	0
5-6	Change Runbooks	1	9	10	9	10	0	0
6-7	Route Runbooks for Approval	1	10	11	10	11	0	0
7-8	Place Runbooks into Production	1	11	12	11	12	0	0

Figure 6-5 A Nonconstruction Activity Time Chart

tivity could be prolonged without extending a project's final completion date.

To calculate the Total Float, subtract the duration and Earliest Start time from the Latest Finish time for each activity. Thus,

Total Float = Latest Finish - Earliest Start -Duration

Ronaldson, for example, calculates the Total Float for "Preparing Access to Roads." He obtains a Total Float of 3 days, which is determined as follows:

3 days = 4 days - 0 days - 1 day
(Total Float) = (Latest Finish) - (Earliest Start) - (Duration)

USING A CHART
FOR NONCONSTRUCTION PROJECTS

The use of an activity time chart is not, of course, limited to construction projects.

For example, an insurance firm wanted to modify some programs to a software system that processed pension payments. According to Figure 6-5, seven activities had to be performed. The project manager repeated the very same steps Ronaldson performed in his construction project.

The project manager computed the start, finish, and float times for each activity using the activity time chart in Figure 6-5. Once the calculations are completed, the project manager is ready to proceed to the next step: determining the critical path.

First, however, in order to get a firm grasp on what has been discussed so far, fill out Planning Page 5 in Appendix B.

7

THE FINAL STEP—THE CRITICAL PATH METHOD

The final step in scheduling a complex project is to determine the critical path through the network diagram. The critical path is a continuous chain of activities deemed critical for the completion of the project. It commences at the very first node of the diagram and ends at the final one.

Determining the critical path helps you set priorities for activities. A delay of the activities on the critical path may adversely affect the duration of the project even though the activities in the path may comprise only 10 to 15 percent of all project activities. You determine the critical path by finding the longest string of events flowing through the diagram, normally located in the center of it.

You can also use a more standardized approach to determine the critical path. Critical path activities must occur at a particular point in time; there is no flexibility available for that occurrence. By looking at the activity time chart in Figure 6-3, you can determine exactly which activities make up the critical path by seeing if, for any particular activity, the Earliest Start equals the Latest Start, the Earliest Finish equals the Latest

Finish, and the duration for the activity equals the difference between the Latest Finish time and the Earliest Start time.

Thus, the criteria for determining those activities located on the critical path are:

Earliest Start time = Latest Start time
Earliest Finish time = Latest Finish time
Duration = Latest Finish time - Earliest Start time

All three criteria must be met if an activity is to be considered on the critical path.

Apply these criteria to the activities listed on the activity time chart, and answer "yes" or "no" for each of the requirements above. Do the same for an activity time chart based on your own project. Appendix C has a chart, or matrix, that is an effective worksheet for this purpose.

As you can see, the following activities belong on the construction project's critical path:

Activity	i-j
Clear Site	1-2
Conduct Survey	2-3
Rough Grade	3-4
Transport Tools to Site	4-7
Transport Crane to Site	7-8
Assemble Crane	8-9
Excavate for Sewer	9-10

The activities on the entire network diagram are tested in this way, and the components of the critical path determined. The project manager can then concentrate on those activities crucial to the completion of the project, knowing if they are delayed, the entire project will be delayed.

ONCE THE DIAGRAM IS COMPLETE

After you complete and refine your own diagram, including an indication of the critical path on it, have it reviewed by

those who attended your inital meeting. This action will secure everyone's approval for the diagram and ensure that you
incorporated all their inputs. It will also reinforce the others'
sense of participation in the overall project.

Once you receive their approval or incorporate their suggestions, distribute a copy of the network diagram to everyone
who needs it. To facilitate your decision on who should receive
the diagram, use the documentation distribution matrix that
you developed earlier.

AN ALTERNATIVE/SUPPLEMENT TO CPM

As a supplement or alternative for a CPM network diagram,
project managers in some industries produce what is known
as an implementation schedule. It is simply a table identifying
the activities required to reach the objectives of the project, in
logical sequence, with their accompanying resource requirements and estimated dates.

The implementation schedule should include information like:

- project title/number
- project manager
- current date
- activity/phase titles
- responsible persons
- estimated costs (labor, equipment, material, and other)
- estimated dates (starting and finish)

The form is especially useful for managers of data processing projects. It serves as a quick means for determining the
dates and costs of each activity or phase. In addition, many
participants feel this form is better than a CPM network diagram because it is easier to read.

8

USING SCHEDULING INFORMATION FOR CALENDARING AND ALLOCATING RESOURCES

Once the network diagram is drawn and the schedules are determined, you need to translate the scheduled workdays into calendar days and allocate resources according to the schedule you develop.

Calendaring involves assigning a scheduled workday to a specific calendar day. For example, Figure 8-1 shows how it would work for a month of January that begins on a Sunday. The "x" under Saturdays and Sundays indicates no workday.

Once you repeat this task for all the activities within the project, you develop a chart indicating exactly on what calendar day the Earliest Start and Earliest Finish dates occur for each activity. For instance, on the activity time chart for our case history, project manager Ronaldson substitutes actual calendar dates for the Earliest Start and Earliest Finish of each activity and lists them with each activity's duration and total float (see Figure 8-2). The procedure is to determine that for the first activity, the Earliest Start and Earliest Finish require a duration of two workdays and require the first two available calendar days (being the first activity). Thus, the Earliest Start

January 19XX							
	S	M	T	W	Th	F	S
Calendar Day	1	2	3	4	5	6	7
Workday	x	1	2	3	4	5	x
Calendar Day	8	9	10	11	12	13	14
Workday	x	6	7	8	9	10	x
Calendar Day	15	16	17	18	19	20	21
Workday	x	11	12	13	14	15	x
Calendar Day	22	23	24	25	26	27	28
Work Day	x	16	17	18	19	20	x
Calendar Day	29	30	31				
Work Day	x	21	22				

Figure 8-1 Example of Calendaring

and Earliest Finish dates for Clear Site are January 2 and January 3, respectively. Then translate the workdays to calendar days for the next activity, and so on. Whenever the duration of an activity changes or the sequences of activities change, the workdays must be revised into different calendar days for the activities.

ALLOCATING RESOURCES

A chief objective of a good project manager is to ensure all activities have the optimum level of resources necessary to complete the project. Those resources include labor, equipment, and materials. To ensure that sufficient resources are available, you must have an objective way to allocate them.

Going to our case history, let us see as an example how Ronaldson determines labor resource requirements for each of the first ten activities. You can apply the same principles when

i-j	Description	Duration (days)	Total Float	Earliest Start	Earliest Finish
1-2	Clear Site	2	0	Jan. 2	Jan. 3
1-5	Prepare Access to Roads	1	3	Jan. 4	Jan. 4
2-3	Conduct Survey	2	0	Jan. 4	Jan. 5
3-4	Rough Grade	1	0	Jan. 6	Jan. 6
4-7	Transport Tools to Site	1	0	Jan. 9	Jan. 9
5-6	Transport Huts to Site	1	3	Jan. 2	Jan. 4
6-7	Prepare Concrete Mixing Area	1	3	Jan. 3	Jan. 6
7-8	Transport Crane to Site	1	0	Jan. 10	Jan. 10
8-9	Assemble Crane	2	0	Jan. 11	Jan. 12
9-10	Excavate for Sewer	2	0	Jan. 13	Jan. 16

Figure 8-2 Earliest Start and Finish Dates per Activity

dealing with your own labor requirements. Subsequently, you'll find his equipment resource method helpful as well. It too can be tailored to your needs.

ALLOCATING LABOR RESOURCES

On a copy of the network diagram, Ronaldson notes the duration of the activity and the estimated number of people needed to complete that activity over the line of each activity arrow. Thus, "Clear Site" (1-2) takes 2 days to complete and requires 10 workers per day. Ronaldson repeats this task for each activity. The part of the network diagram that is our example then looks like this (see Figure 8-3).

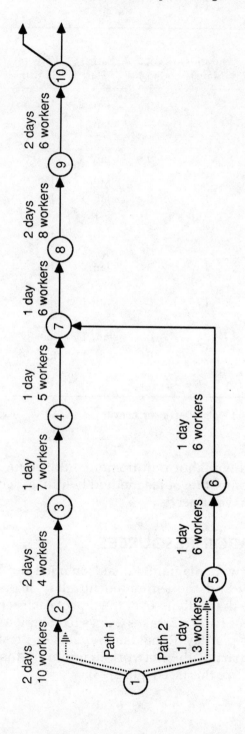

Figure 8-3 CPM Diagram Showing Labor Requirements for Each Activity

Path 1 = Critical Path
Path 2 = Noncritical Path

How does the project manager know how many people to assign to each activity? This decision is based on the input received during the meeting held to develop a preliminary network diagram. Other ways for a project manager to make this determination is to estimate based on historical data gathered from previous projects, or to make a "best guess" based on previous personal experiences. One of the advantages of using estimates gathered at the meeting, however, is that they already have the support of the major participants, and again provide valuable reinforcement to their "proprietorship" of the project.

The indication on the diagram of the critical and noncritical paths will later help to determine which activities will have higher priority in receiving labor resources and how to supply the critical activities with workers who have the necessary skills for each. Figure 8-4 is an additional diagram, taken from the case history. This one is a histogram reflecting the total number of people and days required for each activity. Ronaldson has drawn this chart for all the activities in the project. (Note this is a rough draft not drawn exactly to scale.)

The vertical axis (Y-axis) is an arithmetic scale to indicate the number of workers necessary to complete the project. On the horizontal axis (X-axis) is an arithmetic scale to indicate the number of days to complete the project. This enables the project manager to put in bar chart form the number of workers and days required for each critical activity, after which the bars for noncritical activities are put in. Therefore, you can be reasonably sure that the bars lying closest to the horizontal axis are the ones indicating the critical activities.

Preparing a Labor Requirements Chart

Once the histogram is complete, use it to develop a labor requirements chart as shown in Figure 8-5. This chart shows the number of workers required for each activity on a specific workday. For example, Ronaldson knows—based on information in the histogram he has made—that the first day will re-

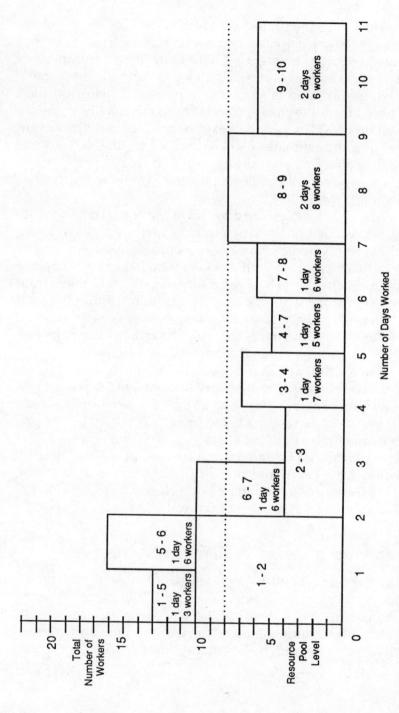

Figure 8-4 Labor Requirement Bar Chart for Each Activity

Activity	1	2	3	4	5	6	7	8	9	10	11
Clear Site (1-2)	10	10									
Conduct Survey (2-3)			4	4							
Rough Grade (3-4)					7						
Transport Tools to Site (4-7)						5					
Prepare Access to Roads (1-5)	3										
Transport Huts to Site (5-6)		6									
Prepare Concrete Mixing Area (6-7)			6								
Transport Crane to Site (7-8)							6				
Assemble Crane (8-9)								8	8		
Excavate for Sewer (9-10)										6	6
Total Labor Required	13	16	10	4	7	5	6	8	8	6	6

Time in days

Figure 8-5 Labor Requirements Chart

quire a workforce of 13 to complete the two activities, "Clear Site" and "Prepare Access to Roads." It's apparent that workforce usage peaks on the second workday, with a 16-worker requirement, and reaches a low on the fourth day, with a 4-worker requirement.

Such peaks and valleys are not reflections of good labor management, however. In a situation like that, the manager will spend too much time trying to find the right number of people for each day, constantly hiring and laying off employees. This is hardly cost-effective in the long run. The object is to keep the labor requirement as even as possible. This is known as leveling.

To level, initially determine the average daily labor requirement for the entire set of a project's activities. You do this by adding total labor requirement sums for each column on the labor requirements chart and dividing that sum by the total time in days for the entire activity. We'll use the example shown in Figure 8-5. Although it does not cover the entire case project, it will serve to demonstrate the method, and you can then apply the procedure to your own projects.

The total workforce for all workdays combined equals 89 workers:

$$89 \text{ workers} = 13 \text{ (workers)} + 16 + 10 + 4 + 7 + 5 + 6 + 8 + 8 + 6 + 6$$

The total number of workdays is 11. The average daily labor requirement is 8:

$$8 \text{ workers} = 89 \text{ workers divided by 11 workdays}$$

Recalculating Labor Requirements

Draw a dotted line on the histogram to reflect the average of 8 workers. Although some days will require more, some fewer, it is now clear that the project manager can maintain a resource pool level of 8 workers. On days when more than eight are needed, the project manager could either subcontract for more or hire temporary employees.

Another course is to alleviate such actions by rescheduling certain activities so that all workday labor requirements come close to matching the average daily labor requirement of 8. Choose those activities having a total float time; schedule them with those critical activities having a labor requirement less than the average daily labor requirement, and which occur within their latest finish time. In this way, the project is not substantially affected.

The histogram, revised accordingly, is shown in Figure 8-6. Three noncritical activities, each having a total float time—"Prepare Access to Roads" (1-5), "Transport Huts to Site" (5-6), and "Prepare Concrete Mixing Area" (6-7)—have been combined with different critical activities. Compare the histogram in Figure 8-4 with the one in Figure 8-6 to see the difference.

Redrawing the histogram enables you to develop a new labor requirements chart (see Figure 8-7) reflecting the new labor requirements for each workday. Here also is the place to update the scheduling information for the network diagram.

Finally, review the labor pool to determine whether workers with the necessary skills are available to complete each activity. If so, they would be assigned to the critical activity first. If there is not sufficient labor with the necessary skills, assign those that *are* available from the resource pool to the critical activity and supplement them through temporary employment services or subcontractors.

The remaining workers in the resource pool are then assigned to the less critical or noncritical activity, if required. For instance, Ronaldson needs four people for the activity labeled "Conduct Survey." However, his records indicate that only three employees in the resource pool are skilled in using surveying equipment. Ronaldson therefore contacts a temporary employment service to obtain the fourth worker. He can then assign those remaining in the resource pool to the activity, "Prepare Access to Roads."

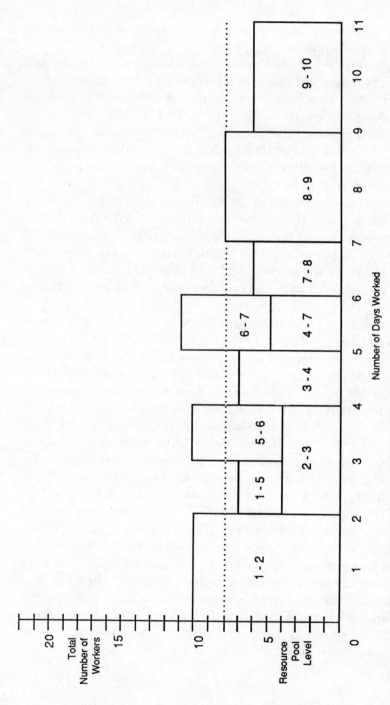

Figure 8-6 Labor Requirements Bar Chart for Each Activity (Leveled)

Activity	1	2	3	4	5	6	7	8	9	10	11
Clear Site (1-2)	10	10									
Conduct Survey (2-3)			4	4							
Rough Grade (3-4)					7						
Transport Tools to Site (4-7)						5					
Prepare Access to Roads (1-5)	0		3								
Transport Huts to Site (5-6)		0		6							
Prepare Concrete Mixing Area (6-7)			0			6					
Transport Crane to Site (7-8)							6				
Assemble Crane (8-9)								8	8		
Excavate for Sewer (9-10)										6	6
Total Labor Required	10	10	7	10	7	11	6	8	8	6	6

Time in days

Figure 8-7 Labor Requirements Chart (leveled)

ALLOCATING EQUIPMENT RESOURCES

It's often possible to use a similar procedure to determine the equipment resources for a project. Ronaldson, for example, can calculate the number of 2 1/2-ton flatbed trucks required daily for each activity in his NCC project. He would start by constructing a network diagram, but labeling each arrow with the duration and the estimated number of trucks necessary to complete the activity. The activity "Conduct Survey" (2-3), for example, takes two days to complete and requires one truck per day. Ronaldson repeats this task for each activity.

After drawing the network diagram, he would develop a resource requirements chart listing the resource requirements and duration for each activity, and whether an activity is on the critical path and thus has priority to receive resources before other concurrent activities.

Ronaldson then calculates the average daily resource requirements by multiplying each resource requirement by the number of days it is needed and totaling the answers, and adding the number of days they will be used.

The average daily requirement for the NCC project is 3 trucks, and is calculated in the following way:

$$\frac{\Sigma \text{ Total Resource Requirement}}{\Sigma \text{ Number of Days}} \quad \frac{35}{14} = 2.5 \text{ trucks}$$

where Σ means "summation of"

Since there is no such thing as 2.5 trucks, Ronaldson would round the figure to the next whole number, 3. Ronaldson therefore keeps a resource pool of 3 trucks at all times. If an activity requires more than 3, he rents or borrows the additional vehicles for the duration of the activity. For instance, "Transport Tools to Site" requires 5 trucks, so Ronaldson orders 2 additional trucks for one day.

Occasionally, two activities occur simultaneously. According to Figure 8-8, for instance, "Clear Site" is concurrent with "Prepare Access to Roads" and "Transport Huts to Site."

Activity (i–j)	Duration (a)	Daily Requirement (b)	Total (a × b)	Lead Ordering Time
Clear Site (1-2)	2	0	0	0
Conduct Survey (2-3)	2	0	0	0
Rough Grade (3-4)	1	0	0	0
Transport Tools to Site (4-7)	1	0	0	0
Prepare Access to Roads (1-5)	1	400 sq. feet	400 sq. feet	3 weeks
Transport Huts to Site (5-6)	1	0	0	0
Prepare Concrete Mixing Area (6-7)	1	350 sq. feet	350 sq. feet	2 weeks
Transport Crane to Site (7-8)	1	0	0	0
Assemble Crane (8-9)	2	100 sq. feet	200 sq. feet	1.5 weeks
Excavate for Sewer (9-10)	2	0	0	0

Figure 8-8 Materials Requirements Chart

Under such circumstances, Ronaldson first allocates the 3 trucks in the resource pool to the critical activity, "Clear Site," and then to the other activities. If "Clear Site" no longer requires any or all the trucks, he assigns them to one or both of the noncritical activities.

When allocating equipment resources, follow these rules:

1. All critical activities have priority over noncritical activities.
2. Shift excess equipment resources to lower priority concurrent activities.
3. Behind-schedule critical activities take precedence over any concurrent noncritical activities in allocating equipment resources.
4. In deciding which noncritical activities have priority, assign resources to the most difficult, most recent, or most uncertain one.

ALLOCATING MATERIAL RESOURCES

Determine the material allocation requirements for each activity by developing a material requirements chart like the one shown in Figure 8-8.

The chart is not as elaborate and in-depth as those for labor and equipment resource requirements. This is because material requirements vary considerably from one activity to another. According to Figure 8-8, for instance, "Clear Site" does not require lumber, while "Prepare Concrete Mixing Area" requires 350 square feet of it. There is not a consistent demand for the lumber.

The chart should contain a column for lead ordering times for each activity. According to his chart, Ronaldson must order 400 square feet of lumber three weeks prior to the earliest start time for "Prepare Access to Roads." He must also submit advance orders for lumber for two other activities, "Prepare Concrete Mixing Area" and "Assemble Crane."

Because material resources are usually not reusable, unlike labor and equipment, the project manager must place a separate order for each activity, whether it is critical or noncritical. Occasionally, materials remaining from one activity may be used for another, to conserve materials and ultimately decrease costs.

In circumstances where it is necessary to determine which of two or more activities must receive resources first, follow these rules:

1. Allocate resources to the activity with the lower i-j designation, and/or
2. Allocate to the activity with the longest duration, and/or
3. Allocate to the most critical activity first and then the noncritical ones, and/or
4. Allocate the most complex activity.

Unless you're beginning a new project or in the midst of an old one, Planning Page 6 in Appendix B will be tough to fill out with specific numbers. But it will help to give you an idea how the entire resource allocation process is carried out.

9

ESTABLISHING A MONITORING SYSTEM FOR PROJECTS

By establishing ways to track the course of all activities and events in the project, you can control, or monitor it. A change in one or more of the many factors involved can alter the course of the entire project. Some of the factors that could change are:

- specifications
- weather conditions
- construction methods
- resource requirements
- budgeting consideration
- project completion date
- working conditions
- availability of workers with necessary skills
- absenteeism
- management
- the economy

Some of those changes will have a pronounced impact on your project. Others could have a more subtle one. Either way, the changes could affect the project in terms of quality and time. Some changes causing delays are excusable— they're not blamed on the contractor. These are usually the ones not attributable to a specific individual or organization. For instance, a labor strike against NCC or a fire destroying the basic structure of a building would be considered excusable delays.

Other delays, however, are not excusable. These are delays that can be directly attributed to neglect by the contractor. For instance, if NCC failed to coordinate the efforts of subcontractors in performing framework or if NCC failed to furnish a sufficient number of workers to complete an activity, the contractor would be responsible for inexcusable delays. The result: either penalty payments or a termination of contract agreements.

But Pacific Realty Associates also has an interest in seeing that the project avoids or overcomes delays caused by change. This firm has set a specific completion date. On that date, it plans to begin moving furniture, equipment, and personnel into the two-story building. Pacific Realty Associates, therefore, has a special interest in making sure that all delays, existing and potential, are detected early so NCC can take remedial action.

Many sources of information can indicate whether a delay will affect a particular activity, including revised drawings, amended specifications, minutes, correspondence, inspection reports, daily construction reports, and many others. But to fully capture this information and to assess whether a delay will occur, you must establish a means for monitoring project activities.

MONITORING PREPARATION

Monitoring requires you to collect data on the actual progress of your project and to verify whether the effort is progressing in conformance with plans. (For our purposes, monitoring means the same as controlling.) With that data, you attempt to detect any deviations or variances that occur and to develop a way to compensate for or correct such activity so as to meet the project completion date.

Here are some of the actions you must take to monitor a project:

- develop procedures for coordinating and integrating the activities of the project participants
- establish effective communication channels
- assess the impact of problems and delays
- determine the adequacy of resources devoted to the project
- obtain reliable information on the status of the project
- assess accurately project costs
- measure project status and accomplishments
- compare current progress to projections and standards

FEEDBACK

The key to effective monitoring is to develop ways to obtain adequate feedback on the progress of a project. Feedback provides the project manager with the information needed to keep the project moving according to schedule. The more feedback that is available, the better the monitoring process.

By comparing data on current status to the project's planned progressions, you can detect exceptions, or variances, in that progress. A variance is usually defined in terms of a scheduling or budgeting deviation.

Variances are generally negative indicators that can be measured quantitatively. When you detect a variance, you must immediately work to develop alternatives that will adequately reduce or eliminate it so as not to interfere with your ultimate goal: the project completion date.

In general, you can set up three criteria as yardsticks to monitor a project: scheduling, resource utilization, and budgeting. Each provides you with an effective way to detect variances. We will discuss them in detail in the next three chapters, but first, here is a quick overview.

SCHEDULE MONITORING

When you monitor a project to determine if everything is proceeding as scheduled, you collect data to detect the type of problems you'll find in Planning Page 9, Appendix B.

Once you collect such information, you can perform a series of actions to rectify the situation. For example, you can update the schedule by reassessing the duration of specific activities. Or, you can resequence or eliminate activities reflected in the current version of your Gantt chart or CPM diagram.

RESOURCE MONITORING

A project usually depends on three resources: labor, materials, and equipment. Without close tracking and control, the costs of utilizing these resources are likely to escalate.

You have basically three tools for tracking resource utilization: meetings, inspections, and forms. Meetings enable you to acquire information rapidly. Inspections allow you to witness what and how certain resources are being used by your project people. Forms allow you to determine quantitatively the extent of the resources being used and the costs associated with using them. In addition, forms serve as an excellent historical record on what occurs throughout the project.

BUDGET MONITORING

When you monitor a project to determine if everything is proceeding according to budgeting plans, your aim is to determine the overall financial condition of the project. You accomplish this by detecting quantitative variations at any given point in time, either for a specific activity or the entire project.

You accumulate cost data from a series of sources, usually related to labor, materials, overhead, and other charges. Compare the actual accumulated data for a particular activity or the entire project with the estimated costs. Analyze any difference or variances and take actions such as curtailing resources devoted to a project or selecting alternative materials.

To monitor the project effectively, you must study its progress on a constant basis. If you find a deviation, analyze it immediately to determine its ultimate effect on the schedule.

The three Planning Pages, 7, 8, and 9, in Appendix B will help you set up a general framework for monitoring schedules, costs and resources. Later, we shall provide specific forms for accomplishing each task.

10

USING NETWORK DIAGRAMS AS MONITORING TOOLS FOR SCHEDULING

The Gantt chart and the CPM network diagram are the two best-known tools to monitor the scheduling of a project. Depending on how they are employed, either can provide a convenient way to assess project progress.

MONITORING BY GANTT

The Gantt chart has one major advantage as a monitoring tool: it is very simple and effective for illustrating the progress or status of an entire project or its individual phases. The Gantt chart is an especially effective tool for conveying information to nontechnical professionals and managers.

You use the open lower portion of the solid black bars to reflect the percent of progress of each phase. Use colored pens or simply slanted lines to fill in the "completed" portion.

For conveying in-depth information on the progress of projects, however, a Gantt chart has some shortcomings, because bar charts do not indicate interdependencies.

Ronaldson, for example, would find it difficult to assess the impact on the masonry phase of a delay in the concrete phase.

The Gantt chart also does not indicate which phases have activities located on the critical path, yet these are the activities that can delay the crucial completion date if they fall behind schedule. It is just as difficult to discern the noncritical activities on a Gantt chart, so you could become alarmed without cause by the impact of a delay on the project completion date.

USING A CPM NETWORK DIAGRAM TO MONITOR

The CPM network diagram, unlike the Gantt chart, provides enough detailed information to assess the effect of a delay associated with any particular phase or activity. The CPM diagram provides more "micro" information than "macro" information; that is, it provides more specific information to evaluate the progress of a project.

Like Gantt, the CPM diagram reflects the percentage of completion for any specific activity. Use a thick bold line over those arrows that have been completed, or over the portion of an activity arrow indicating the percent completed.

To update CPM diagrams, you need up-to-date information. Otherwise, your diagram becomes merely a historical document rather than a useful tool. You can collect information from many sources, particularly from existing documentation, meetings, and word-of-mouth.

In regularly scheduled meetings, the project manager has access to information that might not be recorded on paper, such as evaluative judgments on whether a specific activity can actually be accomplished in a certain way.

WRITTEN SOURCES FOR MONITORING

Change orders are one written source of information. You can see one in Appendix C. You can keep track of change orders by maintaining a log on all those occurring in the project, listing entry number, change order number, who requested it, who authorized it, who accepted it, the effective date and the affected activity.

By using the information in these documents, you can determine which activities are affected by the change order and the degree to which the change order influences them.

Many project managers also keep a record of project delays to help them update their network diagram. With it, you can record delays and other pertinent information, including activity description, date delay reported, reason for the delay, and so forth.

The record of project delays helps in two ways. You keep track of the delays that have occurred, and you develop a historical record to refer to when you revise the network diagram and schedules.

OTHER MONITOR REPORTS

There are other sources you can tap. Ronaldson, for example, reviews documentation on his NCC project, like Daily Construction Reports, to determine whether an activity can meet its finish date and whether a delay will affect the final completion date. He also obtains necessary information from inspections and other reports.

As project manager, Ronaldson prepares a weekly document titled the Activity Status Report. An example of one is shown in Figure 10-1. He distributes this document to all project participants, referring to his document distribution matrix. This record enables everyone to see the status of his or her phases at the end of any particular week.

The document is also useful to determine if an activity will be behind or is behind schedule. In Figure 10-1, you can see that the activity "Transport Tools to Site" is only 50 percent complete as of January 6, the date it should have been done. To investigate this kind of situation, the project manager must talk with various participants and review the project

PHASE _____ Site Work

Activity	i-j	Duration (days)	Estimated Actual Completion Date	Total Float	% Complete	Remaining Duration
Clear Site	1-2	2	Jan. 2	0	100	0
Prepare Access to Roads	1-5	1	Jan. 2	3	100	0
Conduct Survey	2-3	2	Jan. 4	0	100	0
Rough Grade	3-4	1	Jan. 5	0	100	0
Transport Tools to Site	4-7	1	Jan. 6	0	50	.5
Transport Huts to Site	5-6	1	Jan. 3	3	100	0
Prepare Concrete Mixing Area	6-7	1	Jan. 4	3	0	0
Transport Crane to Site	7-8	1	Jan. 7	0	0	1
Assemble Crane	8-9	2	Jan. 10	0	0	2

Figure 10-1 Activity Status Report

PHASE   Pension Enhancements

Activity	i-j	Duration	Estimated Actual Completion Date	Total Float	% Complete	Remaining Duration
Design Interface	1-2	2	Jul 3	0	100	0
Conduct Walkthrough	1-3	1	Jul 5	1	100	0
Modify Programs	2-4	5	Jul 12	0	30	1
Run Tests	4-5	2	Jul 16	0	50	1
Change Runbooks	5-6	1	Jul 17	0	0	1
Route Runbooks for Approval	6-7	1	Jul 18	0	0	1
Palce Runbooks into Production	7-8	1	Jul 19	0	0	1

Figure 10-2 Nonconstruction Activity Status Report

documentation. In this case, Ronaldson finds that this activity has no total float and, therefore, will require him to reschedule the activity to some degree.

NONCONSTRUCTION ACTIVITY STATUS REPORT

An Activity Status Report can be adapted to your own project; it is not limited to construction projects. The insurance company that we saw in Chapter VI trying to modify some programs to a software system that processes pension payments is now going one step further.

Its project manager produces a weekly Activity Status Report like the one in Figure 10-2. It is based on the information contained in its network diagram and Activity Time Chart which you saw back in Figure 6-3. Like Ronaldson, the insurance project manager is concerned with monitoring the status of each activity and performs the very same steps.

For instance, the activity "Modify Programs" is only 80 percent complete on July 12, the date it should have been done. The project manager investigates the discrepancy to determine the source of the delay and to take the appropriate action.

Planning Page 10 in Appendix B will help you get started in your schedule monitoring activities. If you don't have specific information from a current project, go back to an old one and see if you can fill out the questions appropriately.

11

COLLECTING INFORMATION TO MONITOR LABOR, MATERIAL AND EQUIPMENT UTILIZATION

Information about the ongoing work of the project reaches the project manager in three general ways: through documentation, meetings and onsite inspection.

USING DOCUMENTATION TO COLLECT INFORMATION

Good forms give the project manager an excellent means of feedback and a convenient way of making reports on the progress of the project, specifically in the three important areas of labor, material and equipment utilization. Visual forms at the work site—charts and graphs—are especially useful in keeping everyone involved up to date on the progress of the work and reinforcing the feeling on the part of all the participants that they have an active stake in the project.

In addition to forms previously described, there are some that are especially suited for providing information that helps the project manager monitor each of the above areas.

COLLECTING INFORMATION ABOUT LABOR UTILIZATION

On the NCC project, project manager Ronaldson finds that two forms are useful in providing him with the information he needs on labor utilization. One is the Daily Time Report. Completed each day by the supervisor in charge of site work on each individual activity, it gives Ronaldson at a glance the employee's name and badge number, the clock hours worked that day and the number of regular and overtime hours, and any remarks the supervisor wants to make. A copy of the daily time report is in Appendix C.

Once the form is completed, the supervisor sends it to the project's timekeeper. The timekeeper compiles the data daily by tallying up the figures for each worker and for each activity and computing a labor cost for each activity.

The information on the form enables the project manager to calculate the unit labor cost and to determine the overall costs to complete an activity. It also provides a historical record to help in determining labor requirements in the future and to predict more accurately the labor costs associated with completing a specific activity.

The Daily Construction Report breaks each activity's labor utilization down into employment categories and provides space for other aspects of the project, such as inspections from state or federal officials, delays in activities, and delivery of significant materials.

The project superintendent completes this report and submits it to Ronaldson's office at the conclusion of each day. The remarks section is for noting any special events that occurred on that day. A sample of the Daily Construction Report used on the NCC project is in Appendix C. Similar forms can be devised for nonconstruction projects showing how employee time is being utilized on each activity.

These daily reports, or adaptations of them, provide the project manager with a constant flow of information on the status of the project. They show at a glance what has occurred, what was accomplished, who accomplished what, and what labor was required for each activity. In addition, any serious delays can be detected quickly and their causes ascertained. They also serve as a "diary" of a project, from its very beginning to its ending. This part of the historical documentation of the project can be used to analyze why certain problems occurred and to determine ways these problems can be overcome in future projects. It also can be used as a positive tool to analyze why certain activities were successful and to determine ways to apply what went right to future projects.

Collecting Information Through Work Orders

The work order is another form that can help you track labor utilization. It communicates which activities will be and are being performed, logs activities, provides useful information to project participants, and formally authorizes the start of an activity. It contains information like:

- project title/number
- activity
- allotted hours to complete the activity
- a description of the work
- actual hours to complete the activity
- actual activity completion date
- the signatures of the individual supervisor, the project superintendent and the project manager.

Once the activity is complete, the person responsible records any applicable information, signs the form, and forwards it to the project manager. For example, on the NCC project, it goes from Ronaldson, who includes the total number of hours to complete the activity and any other pertinent information, like equipment and material requirements, to the project superintendent. The project superintendent signs the document and forwards it to the appropriate supervisor. Once the activity is complete, the supervisor signs the work order and sends it to the superintendent, who reviews it and sends it to Ronaldson for filing.

COLLECTING INFORMATION ON MATERIAL USAGE

A specific system must be installed in a project to track the purchasing of materials in order to avoid excessive buying and ensure that the necessary materials are available. The purchase order (PO) and the Daily Material Report are two methods to develop such a system.

The PO serves several distinct purposes. First, it gives the project manager direct control over the purchasing of material; no one can order anything without his or her consent. Second, it offers a way to track the progress of a project by quickly ascertaining whether a delay in the delivery of materials has occurred or is likely to occur. Third, it provides enough data to compare actual purchase costs with planned purchase costs at any given time.

The Daily Material Report is completed whenever an actual delivery of material is made.

It not only helps track what was actually delivered, but enables the project manager to see whether the material that was delivered actually matches that shown on the invoice and on the purchase order, so that any discrepancies can be communicated to the vendor and rectified.

COLLECTING INFORMATION ABOUT EQUIPMENT UTILIZATION

The use of equipment involves project costs associated with parts, repair services, fuel, and so forth, as well as additional costs that include all the expenses of operating the machine, both direct and indirect.

To record this information, the project manager completes a Daily Equipment Report at the end of each day, and uses it to compare estimated equipment utilization costs with actual utilization for each activity and/or for the entire project. A sample form for this report is in Appendix C.

USING MEETINGS TO COLLECT INFORMATION

Meetings are a crucial means of gathering project information. Here facts that are not clearly defined in paperwork can be brought out through questions and face-to-face explanations. Things that employees may hesitate to commit to paper, or that may be difficult to express in writing can be expressed at a meeting. There is also the obvious advantage of instant feedback.

On the construction project, for example, Ronaldson had become aware that certain activities pertaining to formwork had been delayed, but he was unsure of the reason. The documentation coming through his office seemed vague about the problem. He could probably have found the source of the difficulty by digging through tons of paperwork for hours. But he wanted an instant answer. So he called a meeting and was told by the field people that one of the subcontractors working on the project had been doing a "less than professional job," thereby causing much of the work to be redone.

It is useful to schedule a checkpoint review meeting at the end of each activity. At it, the participants, including the project manager, the supervisor, and others, if applicable, review all documentation related to that particular activity and discuss any variances that may have occurred, how they occurred, and who was responsible for their occurrence. They also discuss the adequacy of the available labor, materials, and equipment resources that were available for the activity and whether enough is available for future activities. As in all meetings, minutes should be taken and distributed according to the documentation distribution matrix.

USING INSPECTIONS TO COLLECT INFORMATION

But the meeting is not the only source of information. Ronaldson knows that onsite inspections can serve his needs well, too. He frequently visits the NCC construction site. But he sometimes is undecided whether to do so unannounced or announced.

He realizes that when he goes unannounced, he can catch the field workers by surprise and see how they actually do their work. But he also knows that this sometimes embarrasses or even alienates everyone, from the project superintendent to the workers. He also knows, however, that if he announces his visits ahead of time, he might not discover where an actual problem exists because the project superintendent or others might cover it up. Throughout his project, Ronaldson ultimately decides to use both announced and unannounced inspections.

PREPARING A PROJECT STATUS SUMMARY

One report that many project managers use to keep abreast of project activities is a periodic project status summary. This is simply a written comment on any discrepancy between the original project completion date and a revised date. It indicates the current status of a project at specific time intervals, such as daily or weekly. The written comments and explanations of delays and overruns should be made graphically explicit with highlighting, arrows, colored symbols, etc., to enhance readability and make the problem areas instantly obvious.

The form works on the same premise as a daily construction report, except that it does not provide as much detailed information. It is like a diary on the course of a project and should be filed in the project history file. Project managers include in the comments section information related to equipment, labor and material utilization. They also include information about any project constraints.

Planning Page 11, in Appendix B, gives you the means to set up a system for your own information collection needs.

12

BUDGET MONITORING

Change orders, inflationary pressures, delays, and other factors lead to escalating costs and budgetary problems. The head of a project needs to have a way to track all the costs associated with each project activity. At specific time intervals, these costs are compiled into reports to help assess the overall cost of the project.

COMPILING LABOR, EQUIPMENT, AND MATERIAL COSTS

Pertinent information on labor, equipment, and material costs is compiled in weekly reports. These weekly reports help determine how efficiently and effectively resources are being used. The project manager can use this information to detect any cost variances that may have occurred, and to take corrective action, such as rescheduling activities or decreasing resource allocations.

On the NCC construction project, an example of the weekly labor cost report is shown in Figure 12-1. Each column lists a different item of important information for each activity.

PROJECT TITLE/NO.: xx-xxx-xx
TYPE OF REPORT: Labor

Week Ending: Jan.14, 19xx
Report No.: 2

(DOLLARS) Activity (i-j)	(a) Original Resource Estimate for Activity	(b) Actual Costs to Date	(c) Percent Activity Complete	(d) Value	(e) Overrun (+) Underrun (−)	(f) Revised Estimate
Clear Site (1-2)	6,000	7,000	100	6,000	+1,000	7,000
Prepare Access to Roads (1-5)	8,000	9,000	100	8,000	+1,000	9,000
Conduct Survey (2-3)	10,000	9,000	100	10,000	−1,000	9,000
Rough Grade (3-4)	6,000	3,000	100	6,000	−3,000	3,000
Transport Tools to Site (4-7)	4,000	5,000	70	2,800	+2,200	6,200
Transport Huts to Site (5-6)	3,000	4,500	60	1,800	+2,700	5,700
Prepare Concrete Mixing Area (6-7)	8,500	6,000	60	5,100	+900	9,400
Transport Crane to Site (7-8)	10,000	4,000	40	4,000	0	10,000
Assemble Crane (8-9)	—	—	—	—	—	—
Excavate for Sewer (9-10)	—	—	—	—	—	—
PROJECT TOTALS	55,500	47,500		43,700	+3,800	59,300

Figure 12-1 Weekly Labor Cost Report

Ronaldson uses this report to assess the resources costs for each activity. It is a composite of the last weekly labor report and all Daily Labor Reports and Daily Construction Reports.

Take as an example the activity "Transport Tools to Site." The original resource estimate cost for the entire activity was $4,000 (column A). By January 14, the activity cost was $5,000 (column B). Yet, the activity is only 70 percent complete (column C). The true cost at 70 percent complete should be $2,800, and this is the figure Ronaldson enters under "Value" (column D).

Obviously, therefore, at the date of the report, January 14, when the activity is 70 percent complete, there is a cost overrun of $2,200 (column B minus column D). So, Ronaldson revises the original resource estimate for the entire activity (column A) by adding the overrrun or underrun in column E to produce the revised resource estimate in column F, which is $6,200. He repeats these steps for each activity.

Ronaldson then assesses the labor resource costs for the project as a whole. For all ten activities combined, the value of the project by January 14 should be $43,700; however, actual costs to date are $47,500. To obtain a revised estimate (column F) for completing all 10 activities, he adds the overrun costs of $3,800 (column E) to the original resource estimate of $55,500 (column A) to obtain a revised estimate of $59,300 for the project (column F).

The format in Figure 12-1 can also be used for material and equipment resource cost reports. Tailor it to indicate a cost breakdown of each type of labor skill, material, or equipment on a per activity and total project basis.

DETERMINING OVERALL PROJECT COSTS

Once each of the required weekly resource reports is completed, they can be combined to determine the overall costs of each activity and the entire project to date, a composite of labor, material, equipment, and overhead costs.

The result of combining these reports on the NCC project is a table like the one on Figure 12-2, a weekly activity cost status report. It is a compilation of the information in each of the weekly resource reports and from any other sources.

To understand Figure 12-2, look at the activity "Transport Tools to Site." The original estimate to complete the activity was $5,000 (column A). The actual cost to date was $6,000 (column B); yet, the activity was only 70 percent complete (column C). To obtain the value (column D), which is the amount the activity should have cost to date, Ronaldson multiplied the 70 percent by the original estimate to complete the activity (column A); the result is a value of $3,500.

He then subtracted the $3,500 (column D) from the actual cost to date (column B) to obtain the amount by which the actual cost to date differs from the value, which is $2,500 (column E). He also included an entry for the previous week's figure on the amount of overrun (column F), which is $2,000. He then subtracted the $2,000 (column F) from the $2,500 (column E) to obtain a difference of $500 (column G).

Ronaldson added the $500 to the previous revised estimate to complete the project, which is $7,000 (column H). That gave him a current revised estimate to complete the activity of $7,500 (column I). Thus, the anticipated cost to complete the activity "Transport Tools to Site" is $7,500 by January 14.

After repeating these steps for each activity, Ronaldson applied them to the project as a whole to date. As shown in Figure 12-2, the original estimate to perform all these activities by January 14 was $73,000 (column A); the actual cost to date was $65,800 (column B). He realized this amount exceeded the estimated cost to date (column D), which is $58,300 (the sum of all amounts in column D). So, he separately added the current week's figures on cost overrun/underrun (column E), last week's figures (column F), and the difference between the two (column G), which are $7,500, $6,550, and $950, respectively. Finally, he added the figures for the previous week's revised estimate ($79,550, column H) and for the new revised estimate ($80,500, column I).

He used this last figure to assess whether the project would ultimately result in a cost overrun or underrun. According to Figure 12-2, the NCC project has a to-date potential cost overrun of $7,500 (column E). Ronaldson added this figure to

PROJECT TITLE/NO.: xx-xxx-xx

TYPE OF REPORT: Activity Cost

Week Ending: May 27, 19xx

Report No.: 2

(DOLLARS) Activity (i-j)	(a) Original Revised Activity Completion Cost	(b) Actual Cost to Date	(c) Percent Complete	(d) Value	(e) This Week's	(f) Last Week's	(g) Difference	(h) Previous Revised Activity Completion Cost	(i) Current Revised Activity Completion Cost
					Overrun(+),Underrun(−)				
Clear Site (1-2)	10,000	11,000	100	10,000	+ 1,000	+ 800	+ 200	10,800	11,000
Prepare Access to Roads (1-5)	12,000	15,000	100	12,000	+3,000	+2,500	+ 500	14,500	15,000
Conduct Survey (2-3)	11,000	8,000	100	11,000	− 3,000	− 2,750	− 250	8,250	8,000
Rough Grade (3-4)	8,000	5,000	100	8,000	− 3,000	− 3,000	0	5,000	5,000
Transport Tools to Site (4-7)	5,000	6,000	70	3,500	+2,500	+2,000	+ 500	7,000	7,500
Transport Huts to Site (5-6)	6,000	9,000	60	3,600	+5,400	+6,200	− 800	12,200	11,400
Prepare Concrete Mixing Area (6-7)	9,000	7,000	60	5,400	+1,600	+ 800	+ 800	9,800	10,600
Transport Crane to Site (7-8)	12,000	4,800	40	4,800	0	0	0	12,000	12,000
Assemble Crane (8-9)	—	—	—	—	—	—	—	—	—
Excavate for Sewer (9-10)	—	—	—	—	—	—	—	—	—
PROJECT TOTALS	73,000	65,800		58,300	+7,500	+6,550	+ 950	79,550	80,500

Figure 12-2 An Activity Cost Status Report

the original estimate to complete the project, which was $1,300,000. That created a current revised project completion cost of $1,307,500.

One of the prime responsibilities of project managers is to determine whether the project is costing or will cost more than anticipated. If that is the case, they must pick up on such cues and take corrective action early. They may have to reschedule activities or reallocate resources to cut costs. Use Planning Page 12 in Appendix B as a formulation for your attempts to monitor budgets.

13

USING THE COMPUTER FOR PROJECT MANAGEMENT

Using a huge mainframe for computerized project management is quickly becoming history. Recent advancements in microcomputing technology, particularly in software, have provided project managers with more affordable tools for automating their project management activities. For example, we have described the construction of a network diagram by manual means, but the same thing could have been done by a computer and, indeed, scheduling is an area where computers are extremely useful.

ADVANTAGES OF USING A COMPUTER

- preparing cost, labor, time, and material estimates quickly
- providing accurate, timely reports
- generating instant answers to queries and problems requiring computations and statistical analysis
- providing alternative paths through a project using countless facts and varying conditions
- forecasting the impact of various approaches to solving a problem or reaching a certain objective

- providing timely cost data in a useful, readable format
- determining immediately how much of a project's total budget has been spent and the amount that will be spent

Output from the Computer

A computer can produce any number of reports with any number of alternatives. It can list information for each activity, i.e.:

- sequence number
- i-j designation
- duration
- earliest start
- earliest finish
- latest start
- latest finish
- total float
- free float
- cost
- priority

It can also generate sorted reports based on such information. For instance, a computer could produce a report listing activities by ascending i-designation of a listing of all activities on the critical path that should occur within a certain time period.

The computer can produce diagrams that reflect varying conditions and facts. Such a capability affords you and other key individuals the opportunity to find the best approach to a project and to determine the ultimate effects of a delay or other problems.

COMPUTER OPTIONS

If you elect to automate all or part of your project management process efforts, you have three basic options. (Four, if you include paying an outside consultant.)

1. You can rent time from another computer owner. This option can prove expensive if extensive processing is required. But it allows your firm to pay only for the time that it uses to do network scheduling. You can use this option if projects are small and infrequent.
2. You can purchase a computer. This option is more expensive than renting time from a computer owner. It is also impractical unless the computer will be used continuously for many projects or will be used for other tasks.
3. You can lease or rent a computer. This option usually fits most needs of a firm. If projects arise intermittently, but are substantial in scope, this option is the best.

Ultimately, the decision to automate network scheduling is based on two factors: frequency and size of projects. If projects are large and occur frequently, you should consider automating your scheduling activities. But if projects are small and occur infrequently, the computerization of scheduling may prove financially impractical. No matter what the size and frequency of your projects, the option of computerization in terms of cost effectiveness should be considered.

There are two Planning Pages in Appendix B for you to complete at this juncture. Planning Page 13 deals with constructing your diagram, and Planning Page 14 will help you assess your need for computerized help.

Microcomputers are Most Feasible

With the introduction of the microcomputer, automation of smaller projects becomes more practical. The microcomputer is the smallest version of business computers. Thanks to advances in microprocessing, these machines process large volumes of information in a short period of time. Although not as powerful as a minicomputer or a mainframe, these machines are perhaps more versatile.

Microcomputers vary in "chip-size" with the most common being 8, 16, and 32 bits. The power of a microcomputer depends on the chip-size; thus, a 16-bit microcomputer is more powerful than a 12-bit one but less powerful than a 24-bit one. Regardless of chip-size, a microcomputer requires at least three chips to operate: one for processing information, another for memory, and another one for interaction with input-output devices like printers. Although not the most powerful, the 16-bit microcomputer is the most popular, partly because of advances in large scale integration.

The Advances of Microcomputers

Because the microcomputer has increasingly taken over from the mainframe or minicomputer the performance of many scheduling activities of medium and large projects, a number of benefits to project managers have resulted.

First, this has reduced the turnaround time for a project management request, such as one to create a network diagram. No longer must managers wait several days for a hard copy of a CPM or PERT schedule. Now, project managers or their staff members can enter data into a microcomputer: within minutes of feeding the information into a microcomputer, they receive their requested report or schedule.

Second, project managers are able to gain better control over the kind of output they receive. For instance, they can specify the content and format of their reports rather than haggle with data processing professionals who sometimes produce output that doesn't conform with the original request.

Third, using a microcomputer rather than a mainframe or minicomputer if the project management software package is not already loaded in a computer is usually more cost-effective. Often firms purchase software for more powerful machines. This can cost tens of thousands of dollars because modifications must be made to the software to meet particular circumstances and charges are assessed for use of the machine's memory. By using a microcomputer for project management, the costs may not be as excessive.

SOFTWARE FOR THE MICROCOMPUTER

For a microcomputer to operate, software, or programs, are needed.

Essentially two kinds of software exist: systems software and application software. Systems software are programs guiding the operation of hardware. Their tasks include monitoring and directing operations, scheduling activities and tasks, and regulating the behavior of input/output devices. This software comprises the operating system of the microcomputer and is stored in the computer's memory.

Various application software programs have been developed. Each enables you to process information in different ways.

Spreadsheet Software

Spreadsheet programs are very popular application software. They allow you to perform mathematical calculations and display data in tabular form. They show a grid of columns and rows. A "cell" is created whenever a row and column intersect. The operator at the machine enters alphanumeric characters in each cell in a format dependent upon the requirements at the time.

These programs are especially useful for calculating and displaying statistical and financial information for a project. For instance, spreadsheet programs may be used to develop change order proposals, implementation schedules, or a record of project delays. Spreadsheet programs can also be used to produce charts, matrices, and tables, such as a documentation distribution matrix, labor requirements chart, or activity time chart. They are also helpful in producing statistical and financial reports, such as weekly labor cost reports or activity cost status reports.

Graphics Software

In addition to spreadsheet programs, several graphics packages are becoming popular among project managers. These programs enable you to display complex data in pictorial form, like pie charts, bar graphs, scatter diagrams, and Gantt charts. Many of these graphic programs enable you to develop free hand displays or to change the size and color of diagrams. Often graphics software are integrated with spreadsheet programs to present data in analytical or presentation form. For example, a graphics package could present voluminous statistical information such as resource requirements and cost data in summary form. One common way to achieve that is to develop a bar chart based upon estimated cost figures at a given date and reflecting actual cost figures of the same date.

These packages offer project managers two advantages. First, they provide a way to present complex data in an easily understood format—graphs. Second, they present an effective overview of a project's status; that is, they make it possible for other project participants to see the "forest before the trees." They can more easily see the relationship of one set of data to another.

Word-Processing Software

Word-processing programs on the microcomputer enable project managers to produce high quality documentation; all kinds of communication, forms, reports and schedules can be created and revised with word-processing software. Some key capabilities of a word-processing package are creating, revising, and deleting documents; inserting, copying, and moving blocks of text throughout a document; changing the format of a character, paragraph, or an entire document; paginating; and archiving documents.

A word-processing package on the project microcomputer offers two principal advantages. First, it usually reduces the turnaround time to produce a document that would be required if it were submitted to a typing pool or word-processing department. Second, it allows project participants to store documents without requiring extensive floor space for tables or file cabinets.

Communications Software

Communications software enable microcomputers to communicate with other computers, whether micro, mini, or mainframe, using a modem that converts digital signals to analog signals and vise versa, via a cable or telephone line. These packages prove to be extremely valuable when a project involves major autonomous operations occurring over a wide geographical area.

Other Software Products

Several other generic types of application software are available for microcomputers operating in the project environment. Some pertain to data base management, compilers, and systems support. With these packages, project managers can apply the power of the microcomputer to do functions relating to accounting, budgeting, calendaring, financial analysis, resource inventory, operations analysis, and purchasing resources.

Project Management Software

The software having perhaps the most impact on project management, regardless of the industry involved, are the project management products. In the last few years, sophisticated software products have been developed to help project managers. These products vary greatly in price and capability. For example, some packages cost several hundred dollars, while others cost several thousand; some packages produce only a simple Gantt chart, while others produce an elaborate network diagram.

Several hundred microcomputer project management packages are currently on the market. Some common packages are:

- Harvard Project Manager™ (Harvard Software, Inc.)
- MicroGANTT® (Earth Data Corporation)

- Microsoft Project®™ (Microsoft)
- Milestone® (Digital Marketing Corporation)
- MPERT™ (Earth Data Corporation)
- Pathfinder™ (Morgan Computing Corporation)
- PC/MIS™ (Davis & Associates)
- Pertmaster™ (Westminster Software, Inc.)
- Primavera Project Planner™ (Primavera Systems, Inc.)
- Project Master™ (Simple Software)
- Project Manager© (Wiley Professional Software)
- Project Reporter© (Cinnamon Microsystems)
- PROMIS™ (Strategic Software Planning Corporation)
- Qwiknet® (Project Software & Development Corporation)
- Superproject™ (Computer Associates Micro Products Division)
- Task Manager™ (Quala)
- Time Line™ (Breakthrough Software)
- Total Project Manager™ (Harvard Software, Inc.)
- Visischedule™ (Paladin VisiCorp.)

The most important element in purchasing a project management software package is knowing what *you* want and need. In Appendix C is a checklist of the various features that are included in some or all project management software programs. Use it as a model for creating your own checklist to guide you in selecting a program that is suited to your own purposes.

Many packages costing only three or four hundred dollars can meet most project management requirements regardless of industry. A less expensive package does not necessarily mean a lower quality of output. At a minimum, however, a project management package should have certain features.

It should allow the development, modification, or deletion of a project. Periodically throughout the project, it should be possible to retrieve the file stored in the microcomputer, update the information, and then generate new reports and diagrams. Therefore, you need a package that allows the development, retrieval, deletion, revision, and storage of all information about your project.

The package should permit development or change of project diagrams. Not all project management software packages produce both a Gantt chart and a network diagram. Frequently, the lower cost packages produce only Gantt charts while the more expensive ones produce a Gantt chart and a network diagram. For Gantt charts, most packages should provide information indicating critical and noncritical activities, major events or "milestones," float time, and possible delays. For network diagrams, they should provide information like critical and noncritical paths; activity titles, their respective start and completion dates, and their duration; and indicate whether an activity has been completed, the percentage of completion, its i-j respective designation, and precedence.

The program should allow development of standard and specialized reports on both detailed and summary levels. The package should permit creation of reports on a specific activity and presentation of information, like its i-j node, duration, early start and finish dates, late start and finish dates, types and amounts of resources required, degree of completion, predecessor activity, next activity, and whether critical or noncritical. Another report that should be included in a project management software package is the resource report indicating per activity start and completion dates, type and amount of resources completed at a specific date, and remaining resources required to complete the activity. In addition, the package should provide you with the capability to produce sorted reports listing activities or events by a specific characteristic such as those having a certain duration, a particular early start or completion date, using a certain resource, or being located on the critical path. These reports can prove extremely helpful in identifying any variances occurring throughout a project.

Project management software should offer some important calendaring capabilities. Perhaps the most important feature is whether you can indicate holidays and vacations. Once you enter this information, the system should automatically adjust schedules accordingly. Most packages have yearly calendars coded into them ranging from 1950 to 2200. In addition, you should be able to specify the length of a work week (5, 6, or 7 days).

A package should have sufficient power to store a substantial number of activities, check for network logic errors, perform resource leveling, and enable "what if" scenarios. A frequent problem, however, with many project management software packages is their requirement for substantial memory to perform tasks such as resource scheduling and "what-if" scenarios. Such requirements necessitate upgrading microcomputers, and this can be costly. An initial investment of $10,000 in software and hardware can quickly double or triple when you upgrade the power of your microcomputer.

If any variation exists in these packages, it is in their capacity to handle a maximum number of activities per project. Most handle a maximum of several hundred activities per project while a few handle several thousand activities. The fact that a package can handle only a few hundred activities per project is not necessarily a drawback. Some packages allow you to divide a project into "subprojects" enabling the storage of several thousand activities. If you want to combine certain projects, you can merge subprojects.

Some programs recognize network logic problems. This feature can prove especially useful in identifying problems in the logic of your network diagram. It can also help prevent "crashing" a program or causing a program to fail to process information and thereby destroy valuable data.

Resource leveling is also important. Without it, the package will conduct scheduling inaccurately because it will ignore the resource constraints of your project. Resources must be proportioned accurately to each activity to meet the anticipated completion date.

"What if" scenarios are crucial, too. With this capability, you can assess the impact a change in information will have on a schedule. For example, you may want to determine what will occur if you change the amount of resources assigned to a specific activity, its duration, its start and completion date, or its position on or off the critical path. A "what if" capability enables you to see how your project will be affected under varying circumstances.

Software packages should not clutter the screen of your microcomputer; that is, they should provide and ask for only essential information. Many project management packages compress too much information on a screen for a given report or graph. For instance, Gantt charts and network diagrams often appear cluttered with information, much of it superfluous. Be sure to review all output on screens for conciseness and clarity. Avoid the mistaken notion that more on the screen is better; otherwise, people using the package could become frustrated and confused.

Most important, the package should allow you to enter the system, store data, generate reports, and view the results on the microcomputer screen. It makes little sense to have a package that requires substantial turnaround time for reports and graphs and produces only hard copies. The package should allow for virtually instantaneous viewing of your efforts.

Be suspicious of advertisements giving the impression that all you have to do is press a button and the necessary graphics and reports will "pop" in front of you. No software package that exists is totally user-friendly. Regardless of package, you must still do some preliminary work before you can use it. You still must identify all activities to complete the project, their interdependencies, who will perform them, and their duration. Then you must load this information into the system, which can be a time-consuming and expensive effort for large projects.

Under most circumstances, using project management software packages on microcomputers is more economical and quicker than using mainframe or minicomputer packages or manually producing schedules and reports. A warning, however, is necessary: avoid thinking these packages are a substitute for good management. A good package will not guarantee success if the project was poorly planned, organized, or controlled in the first place. These packages serve as tools to help you plan, organize, and control your project.

In other words, the software will not do your job but will help you do it better.

You should also develop a checklist to use for almost any type of software: word processing, data communications, data base, spreadsheet, graphics, or project management software. It should include the following questions:

- Will the software satisfy the requirements of the user?
- Is the software user-friendly?
- Will the software require much maintenance?
- Will the software provide needed applications?
- Will the software generate reports in the required format?
- Will the software require much operator intervention?
- Will the software consume much computer time, disk storage, or other resources relative to its capabilities?
- Has the software been widely sold?
- Does the software vendor have a good reputation?
- Is the software product reliable?
- Will the vendor allow you to alter the software?
- Is the reputation of the vendor's service to its customers good?

The questions are basic and should not be ignored if you want quality service and support when using the software. Planning Page 15 in Appendix B can help you formulate your checklist.

In fact, you should make it a rule to develop a checklist for selecting any software to support project management activities. A checklist can help you select the product you need and facilitate your shopping. Once you have a checklist, you will be ready to search for the ideal product. Use the checklist! Do not listen blindly to a vendor; avoid accepting anything at face value. If a salesperson claims a software product meets a certain criterion, ask him or her to demonstrate it or at least guarantee the feature in writing. Ask for nothing less than what is on the checklist. Remember, the vendor is in the business to make money and sometimes may feel compelled to make outrageous claims. To avoid acquiring software that does not meet your requirements or fighting lengthy litigation, insist that each vendor respond with a demonstration—corresponding to the criteria on your checklist.

Also, provide a representative portion of your own data for testing. This will help you decide whether the software meets your exact needs. After the demonstration, you can decide whether to purchase or lease the software.

THE COSTLY IMPACT OF AUTOMATED PROJECT MANAGEMENT

As useful as some of the software we have described may be, you should recognize that automating your project management activities could prove very expensive. The only way to judge its worth to you is to conduct a feasibility study, as described later in this section. First, you obviously need to purchase a microcomputer. Then, in addition to the software, you need to purchase a sufficient amount of supplies, from ribbons to paper. Third, you will need a printer, and for more advanced software products such as project management software, you may also have to purchase a plotter to produce quality graphics. So for just one workstation, automated project management can run into tens of thousands of dollars.

In addition, some hidden costs exist in automated project management. First, you will probably need to develop effective user documentation. For example, you may have to develop a coding manual, user's manual, or operator's manual. This can prove costly and time-consuming. Second, you will probably have to develop and conduct a training program. Unless you hire a staff experienced in using microcomputers, enough time must be devoted to training employees. Effective training uses time in which employees would be attending to their respective project management activities. You must be willing to accept the reality that employees will experience a learning curve before becoming fully productive in using the machine and its accompanying software. Third, security measures will be needed to protect data stored in the machines.

For instance, you will probably need to develop back-up procedures and disaster recovery plans and implement personnel, access, and procedural controls.

Before automating your project management practices, therefore, recognize that some high costs may be involved. Fortunately, you can avoid costly mistakes by first conducting a feasibility study. It will help you determine whether there actually is a need for automating. A feasibility study involves investigating what is currently being done and the time it takes to do it, and determining the available alternatives to meet current and future needs. Then, a cost comparison of each alternative is made, and finally, the best alternative is selected, even if that alternative is the status quo. The feasibility study will help you answer such questions as:

- Is this the right time to automate?
- To what extent should automation be carried out?
- How will automation affect equipment usage, procedural actions, personnel requirements, and your own responsibilities?
- What type of arrangement will best meet your needs?
- How much will automated project management cost?
- Is automated project management really worth it?

AUTOMATING WITH RESTRAINTS

Current advances in software products are having a great influence on project management practices throughout all industries. Project managers have at their disposal a wide assortment of products, ranging from spreadsheet to specialized project management programs. They should be judicious in selecting their software, regardless of their industry. Otherwise, automation can become a costly and time-consuming project in itself. Remember, automation need not be all or nothing. It is possible to automate parts of the project manager's process—the most routine paperwork, for example— without committing to a full, and costly, computerized operation.

A GLOSSARY OF PROJECT MANAGEMENT TERMS

Activity	The work or effort needed to complete a particular event. It consumes time and resources.
Activity Description	An active verb and an object describing the particular activity that an arrow represents. (Example: "clear site" or "assemble crane".)
Activity Description Form	The form used during a meeting to draw a preliminary network diagram. It enables the project manager to record the sequence number, description, duration, starting point, and ending point of each activity included in the network diagram.
Activity Status Record	A document produced by the project manager to show the progress of activities occurring in a project.
Authority	The legitimate power a project manager has to use resources to reach an objective and to exercise discipline.

Average Daily Resource Requirement	The likely amount of resources required to complete an activity or several activities on any workday during a project. The average daily labor requirement is one example.
Backward Pass Method	The method used to calculate the Latest Finish time. It requires reading the network diagram from right-to-left.
Budget Monotoring	Actions by the project manager to determine the costs of a specific activity.
Calendaring	The process of assigning a particular workday to a specific calendar day so that all project participants can relate to the schedules that the project manager creates.
Change Order	A document authorizing a detailed change in the specifications of a project.
Change Order Log	A document used to record the individual change orders that occur during a project. It is especially useful for tracking the processing of a change order.
Checkpoint Review Meeting	A scheduled meeting usually held either at the beginning to discuss goals, targets, and possible problems and contingencies or at the end of an activity to discuss its positive and negative results.
Communications Network	An organized system for sending and receiving data and information.
Consultant Approach	One of the four meeting styles used by the project manager to draw up a preliminary network diagram. This style requires the services of an "objective" consultant to compose the diagram.
Contractor	A firm that agrees to do work for a person or another firm by providing services or supplies according to terms of an agreement.

Controlling	One of the three managerial functions. It requires managers to pursue those actions necessary for ensuring that actual operations happen according to plan.
CPM	Acronym for *Critical Path Method*. A network diagramming technique that places emphasis on time, cost, and the completion of events.
Critical Path	The longest route through a network that contains activities absolutely crucial to the completion of the project.
Critical Path Matrix	A graphic display indicating the three conditions necessary for determining which activities are located on the critical path.
Daily Construction Report	A construction document completed daily indicating what was accomplished and by whom for all occurring activities. Also, it shows labor usage and any special circumstances that could affect the project in any way.
Daily Equipment Report	A document completed daily to record equipment usage for each activity.
Daily Material Report	A report completed daily to record what materials were delivered and by whom.
Daily Time Report	A document used to record the time employees spend on an activity.
Democratic Approach	One of the four meeting styles used by the project manager to draw up a preliminary network diagram. This style requires involvement of as many project participants as possible.
Deviation	A synonym for variance. Anything that strays from a given standard or path.

Documentation Distribution Matrix	A graphic display to help the project manager determine the destination of incoming and outgoing documents during a project.
Dummy Arrow	A dashed line indicating an activity that uses no time or resources.
Duration	The time it takes to complete an activity.
Earliest Finish	The earliest time an activity can be completed.
Earliest Start	The earliest an activity can begin if all activities before it are finished. It is the earliest time that an activity leaves its i-node.
Equipment Department	The organizational unit within a firm responsible for coordinating the use, maintenance, and purchasing of equipment during the different phases of a project.
Estimating Department	The organizational unit within a firm responsible for preparing detailed estimates on the cost of a project.
Event	A synonym for node. A point in time that indicates the accomplishment of a milestone. It consumes neither time nor resources and is indicated whenever two or more arrows intersect.
Excusable Delays	Circumstances that are not attributed to any one person or group, but to an "Act of God" or any other unforeseen happening.
Feedback	The consequences of managerial and organizational actions, plans, and decisions, communicated back to decision-makers so that corrective action can be taken, if necessary. Also, the consequences of employee action made known to the relevant employees so that the individual knows what he or she is doing right, what needs to be

corrected, and that the person's actions count in the overall project.

Fiscal Department	The organizational unit within a firm responsible for providing project cash flow requirements throughout the course of a project.
Forward Pass Method	The method used to calculate the Earliest Start time for each activity in the network diagram. It requires the project manager to assume that the project begins at time zero and that each activity begins immediately after the conclusion of the preceding activity. It also requires reading the network diagram from left-to-right.
Free Float	The amount of time that an activity can be delayed without affecting succeeding activities.
Gantt Chart	A bar chart indicating the time interval for each of the major phases of a project.
Histogram	A synonym for bar chart.
Horizontal Node Numbering	Numbering the nodes of a network diagram in horizontal order, thereby requiring the individual to read the diagram from left-to-right only.
i-designation	The number assigned to the starting point for each activity shown in the network diagram. It represents the head of the arrow.
i-j designation	The unique numbers assigned to each activity indicating the starting and ending points.
Inexcusable Delays	Circumstances that are attributed to negligence on the part of the contractor or subcontractor and produce negative repercussions, such as penalty payments or contract termination.
Inspections	Visits by the project manager at the actual project site. They can be either announced or unannounced.

j-designation   The number assigned to the ending point for an activity shown in the network diagram. It represents the tail of the arrow.

Latest Finish   The latest time an activity can be completed without extending the length of a project.

Latest Start   The latest time an activity can begin without lengthening a project.

Leader Approach   One of the four meeting styles used by the project manager. This style requires only the services of one individual: the project manager. No one else is included in drawing up the diagram.

Leveling   The process of "smoothing" out labor, material, and equipment requirements to facilitate resource allocation. The project manager accomplishes this by "rescheduling" noncritical activities so that the total resource requirements for a particular day match the average daily resource requirements.

Matrix   A graphic display of solutions to problems or situations under varying conditions.

Most Likely Time   Used in PERT diagramming. The most realistic time estimate for completing an activity or project under normal conditions.

Network Review Sheet   An approval sheet distributed to project participants to record their input into an "updated" version of a network diagram.

Network Updating   The process of keeping a network diagram current.

Note   A synonym for event.

Oligarchic Approach   One of the four meeting styles used by the project manager to draw up a preliminary network diagram. This style requires involving only a se-

lect few from among the many project participants.

Optimistic Time	Used in PERT diagramming. The time the firm can complete an activity or project under the most ideal conditions.
Organizing	One of the three managerial functions. It requires managers to design a formal structure of tasks and authority to expedite the company's commitment to reach project objectives.
PERT	Acronym for *Program Evaluation and Review Technique*. A network diagramming technique that places emphasis on the completion of events rather than cost or time.
Pessimistic Time	Used in PERT diagramming. The time the firm can complete an activity or project under the worst conditions.
Planning	One of the three managerial functions. It requires managers to define organizational goals and to determine the means to achieve those goals.
Preliminary Network Diagram	The initial draft of a network diagram depicting the sequence of activities and events occurring in a project.
Project	The overall work or effort being planned. It has only one beginning node and ending node. Between those nodes are countless activities and their respective nodes.
Project Breakdown Structuring	The process of separating a project into definable, major phases.
Project History File	A file or notebook containing all relevant documentation on the planning, organizing, and controlling of a project.

Project Manager | The individual who has overall responsibility for the planning, organizing, and controlling of a project.

Project Phase | A major component, or segment, of a project. It is determined by the process known as project breakdown structuring.

Purchase Order | A documentation authorizing a company to purchase materials from a vendor. It includes a description of the ordered item(s) and the unit price(s).

Purchasing Department | The organizational unit within a firm responsible to determine material requirements and to provide dates for the bidding process.

Record of Project Delays | A document used to record each delay that occurs during a project. Major points of information recorded are the reason for the delay, the activity affected, and whether it will affect the project completion date.

Requirements Chart | A diagram reflecting the resource requirements for each workday during a project. A labor requirements chart is an example of this chart.

Resource Allocation | The processes of determining labor, equipment, and material resource requirements for activities of a project and meeting them with what is available.

Resource Monitoring | Actions by the project manager to determine the amount of resources consumed either for a specific activity or an entire project.

Resource Pool | A group of resources on standby to meet the resource requirements for each workday during a project. Usually equal to the average daily resource requirement.

Responsibility
: The degree of accountability a person has for a particular phase of a project or an entire project.

Revision History Log for Drawings
: A document recording the source, revision description, and outcome for drawings used in a project.

Schedule Monitoring
: Actions by the project manager to determine the status of activities or an entire project at any given point in time.

Scheduling
: The process of determining the starting and ending times for phases and activities of a project.

Sort Report
: A listing of some or all activities in a project according to specific criteria. Usually produced by a computer.

Subcontractor
: A person or firm contracting to perform specialized work for a contractor.

Superintendent
: The individual or firm who has direct responsibility for actual line operations at the project site.

Total Float
: The total amount of flexibility in scheduling activities on a noncritical path. Hence, it provides the time an activity could be prolonged without extending a project's final completion date.

Variance
: A synonym for deviation. Anything that strays from a given standard or path.

Vertical Node Numbering
: Numbering the nodes of a network diagram in vertical order, thereby requiring the individual to read the diagram from top-to-bottom and left-to-right.

Work Breakdown Structuring
: The process of separating major project phases into definable, distinct activities.

Work Flow

A visual display of the flow of a document or the sequence of actions of manual work.

X-axis

The horizontal line on the Gantt chart indicating the appropriate time scale for completing the project.

Y-axis

The vertical line on the Gantt chart listing sequentially the phases of the project.

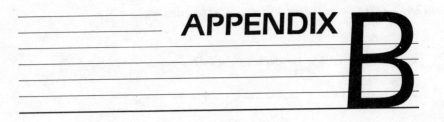

APPENDIX B

PLANNING PAGE 1

DEVELOPING PROJECT PARAMETERS

1. Answer the following general questions so you can start your project on the right course:

    A. What will be accomplished by the project?

    _____

    _____

    _____

    B. How will it be achieved?

    _____

    _____

    _____

C. Where will it be accomplished?

_____

_____

_____

D. When will the project be completed?

_____

_____

_____

E. What major activities will occur and who will perform them?

_____

_____

_____

2. I have the responsibility for

_____

_____

_____

3. I have the authority to

_____

_____

_____

I must go above my level to

_____

_____

_____

_____
_____
_____
_____
_____
_____

PLANNING PAGE 2

PROJECT MANAGER RESPONSIBILITIES

1. Name and describe the principal line functions in your project.

_____

_____

_____

2. Name and describe the principal staff functions of your project.

_____

_____

_____

_____

3. Review your company's organizational chart and list the names of the major participants in your project.

_____

_____

_____

4. Determine those participants with whom you want to maintain constant liaison.

_____

_____

_____

5. List your major planning responsibilities.

_____

_____

_____

6. List your major organizing responsibilities.

_____

_____

_____

7. List your major controlling responsibilities.

_____

_____

_____

_____

_____

_____

_____

_____

_____

_____

PLANNING PAGE 3

DOCUMENTATION AND COMMUNICATION

1. Put the distribution matrix you have made with the planning
    sheet on this page as the first point in your communication net-
    work.

2. List the specific and general manuals that will be used. For each
    manual give a general description of the contents.

Manual   **Description**

_____   _____

_____   _____

_____   _____

_____   _____

_____   _____

3. Determine what should go into the project history file. Also, determine how you will organize the file.

    _____

    _____

    _____

    _____

4. Determine at what intervals you want to hold your scheduled meetings. Decide what you want to achieve at them.

    _____

    _____

5. Determine what sort of occasions would prompt you to call an ad hoc meeting.

    _____

    _____

    _____

_____

_____

_____

_____

_____

_____

PLANNING PAGE 4

THE GANTT CHART AS A
PROJECT MANAGMENT TOOL

1. Break down your major phases.

   _____   _____

   _____   _____

   _____   _____

   _____   _____

2. Estimate the duration for each phase. (The time interval is up to you.)

   _____   _____

   _____   _____

   _____   _____

3. Combine all the information you need to draw a Gantt chart.

    _____

    _____

    _____

4. Determine whether the Gantt chart meets your needs as a descriptive device for your project.

    _____

    _____

    _____

5. Determine who needs a Gantt chart and distribute it accordingly.

    _____   _____

    _____   _____

    _____   _____

_____
_____
_____
_____
_____
_____

PLANNING PAGE 5

PREPARATIONS FOR A NETWORK DIAGRAM

1. Determine the best approach (whether democratic, oligarchic, consultant, or leader) to receive input to construct the network diagram.

    _____

    _____

2. Answer the following questions at your meeting to construct your network diagram:
    a) What activities must be performed?

        _____

        _____

        _____

b) Which activities have a higher priority than others?

_____

_____

_____

c) How many resources are available for each activity?

_____

_____

_____

d) How many resources are required for each activity?

_____

_____

_____

e) Who will perform each activity?

_____

_____

_____

f) Where will the activity be performed?

_____

_____

_____

g) How will the activity be performed?

_____

_____

_____

h) What is the duration of each activity?

_____

_____

_____

_____

_____
_____
_____
_____
_____
_____
_____

PLANNING PAGE 6

ALLOCATING RESOURCES

1. Translate the workdays in your schedule into calendar days.

2. Determine those resources you must allocate for your project.

_____

_____

_____

3. For each resource, do the following:
    Develop a network diagram showing the requirements for each activity.

_____

_____

Develop a histogram reflecting the days and requirements of each activity.

_____

_____

Develop a requirements chart showing the resource needs for each activity.

_____

_____

Determine the average daily resource requirement.

_____

_____

Level your resource allocations and adjust the requirements chart accordingly.

_____

_____

Determine whether you have the right resources to meet the resource requirements for each activity; if not, decide how you will acquire the resources to meet those requirements.

_____

_____

_____
_____
_____
_____
_____
_____
_____

PLANNING PAGE 7

SCHEDULE MONITORING

1. Differences between estimated start dates and actual start dates for each activity.

_____

_____

2. Differences between estimated finish dates and actual finish dates for each activity.

_____

_____

3. The percentage of completion for an activity or the entire project.

_____

_____

4. Unexpected delays or other abnormalities that alter the project's completion date.

_____

_____

5. Activities performed out of network sequence.

_____

_____

6. Milestone activities that appear incapable of being achieved.

_____

_____

_____
_____
_____
_____
_____
_____
_____

PLANNING PAGE 8

COST MONITORING

1. Differences between estimated costs and actual costs for each activity and for the entire project.

_____

_____

2. List any significant deviations.

_____

_____

3. Determine the cause(s) of the variance(s).

_____

_____

4. Decide whether original cost estimates have to be revised.

_____

_____

5. List those activites requiring a revision in their cost estimates.

_____

_____

6. Assess whether the revisions will affect the cost estimate for the entire project.

_____

_____

_____
_____
_____
_____
_____
_____

PLANNING PAGE 9

RESOURCE MONITORING

1. Differences existing between estimated resource requirements and actual resource requirements for each activity and for the entire project.

    _____

    _____

2. List any significant deviations.

    _____

    _____

3. Determine whether the original resource estimates for any particular activity must be revised.

    _____

    _____

4. Determine whether the original resource estimate for the entire project must be revised.

    _____

    _____

5. Determine if the re-estimate of resources will result in a delay in the project.

    _____

    _____

_____
_____
_____
_____
_____
_____
_____

PLANNING PAGE 10

SCHEDULE MONITORING

Note: You may not be able to complete the diagrams directly on this Planning Page, but jot down any notes you need in the blank spaces.

1. Develop a Record of Delays that will meet your project requirements.

_____

_____

2. Use your imagination and develop a log(s) that will help you to track the progress of your project's activities.

_____

_____

3. Develop and complete an Activity Status Report.

_____

_____

4. Complete a Gantt chart showing the percentage of completion for each phase.

_____

_____

5. Complete a CPM network diagram showing the activity completion percentages.

_____

_____

6. Determine who will need a copy of the Activity Status Report and the updated Gantt chart and network diagrams.

_____

_____

_____
_____
_____
_____
_____
_____
_____

PLANNING PAGE 11

COLLECTING INFORMATION

1. Define exacly what you want to monitor in your project.

   _____

   _____

   _____

2. Determine the best ways you can collect information on the status of your project (meetings, inspections, documentation, etc.).

   _____

   _____

   _____

   _____

3. Decide on the forms you need to collect your information.

_____   _____

_____   _____

_____   _____

_____   _____

4. Determine who must complete each form and when it must be completed.

FORM   *RESPONSIBILITY/DUE DATE*

_____   _____

_____   _____

_____   _____

_____   _____

_____   _____

_____
_____
_____
_____
_____
_____
_____

PLANNING PAGE 12

MONITORING BUDGETS

1. List some of the factors that could cause your project to have a cost overrun.

   _____

   _____

   _____

2. Determine the content and format for your weekly labor, material, and equipment cost reports.

   _____

   _____

   _____

   _____

3. Determine the content and format for your weekly activity cost status report.

_____

_____

_____

4. Compile the information from each weekly report and write it in the appropriate place on your activity cost status report.

_____

_____

_____

5. Based on the information in the activity cost status report, determine whether the project has a potential cost overrun or underrun and the amount.

_____

_____

_____

_____
_____
_____
_____
_____
_____
_____

PLANNING PAGE 13

CONSTRUCTING A NETWORK DIAGRAM

1. Construct the final version of the network diagram. Be sure to assign an i-j designation to each activity.

   _____

   _____

   _____

   _____

2. Prepare a schedule based upon the information in the network diagram. You can start by calculating the following times:

   Earliest Start _____

   Earliest Finish _____

Latest Start _____

Latest Finish _____

Free Float _____

Total Float _____

3. Based upon your calculations, define the critical path by constructing a matrix.

_____

_____

_____

_____

_____

_____

_____
_____
_____
_____
_____
_____
_____

PLANNING PAGE 14

ANAYLYZING YOUR NEED FOR A COMPUTER

1. List the advantages of using a computer for your project(s).

   _____

   _____

   _____

2. List the disadvantages of using a computer for your project(s).

   _____

   _____

   _____

3. If you elect to use a computer, define and list the type of input data that will be required.

_____

_____

_____

4. If you elect to use a computer, define and list the output, such as reports, that will be produced by it.

_____

_____

_____

5. If you elect to use a computer, determine the best option to automate your CPM diagramming and scheduling efforts: buying, leasing or renting.

_____

_____

_____

_____

_____

_____

_____

_____

_____

_____

PLANNING PAGE 15

SELECTING SOFTWARE

1. Determine whether you need automated project management by conducting a feasibility study.

    _____

    _____

    _____

2. Determine which categories of software programs you will need.

    _____ Word Processing   _____ Spreadsheet

    _____ Data Base   _____ Graphics

    _____ Graphics   _____ Communications

    _____ Compiler   _____ Systems Support

_____ Project Management

_____ Others: _____

_____

_____

3. For each category of software, determine your requirements.

_____

_____

_____

4. Request a vendor demonstration based upon your requirements.

_____

_____

_____

5. Determine whether you will need to develop in-house documentation, training, and security programs to use your software.

_____

_____

_____

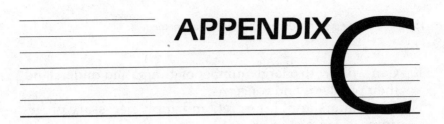

APPENDIX C

SAMPLE FORMS

CHARACTERISTICS AND CAPABILITIES OF A GOOD PROJECT MANAGER

1. Has good general management skills with excellent oral and written communication capabilities.
2. Knows inventory procedures and policies related to materials and equipment.
3. Has a solid background in scheduling and monitoring techniques.
4. Is skilled in gathering data, especially in inverviewing, conducting surveys, examining records, and observing project activities.
5. Understands mathematical and statistical concepts.
6. Has good documentation skills.
7. Has expertise in labor relations and safety procedures.
8. Can ensure that project activities conform to plans and contract requirements.
9. Can adjust to a variety of tasks under constantly changing conditions.

10. Can work with a large number of groups and understand their problems and concerns.
11. Can understand, interpret, and apply necessary procedures to complete a project.
12. Is able to devise methods to control and evaluate project performance.
13. Can engender a spirit of cooperation amoung different participants in a project.
14. Can relate, compare, classify, and evaluate facts.
15. Can distinguish between what is essential and what is nonessential.

SECTIONS OF PROJECT HISTORY FILE

	Applicable	Nonapplicable	Responsibility
Planning Section			
CPM diagrams	⎯⎯	⎯⎯	⎯⎯⎯⎯⎯
Gantt charts	⎯⎯	⎯⎯	⎯⎯⎯⎯⎯
Design documents	⎯⎯	⎯⎯	⎯⎯⎯⎯⎯
Organizing Section			
Organization chart	⎯⎯	⎯⎯	⎯⎯⎯⎯⎯
Project strategy statements	⎯⎯	⎯⎯	⎯⎯⎯⎯⎯
Project goal statements	⎯⎯	⎯⎯	⎯⎯⎯⎯⎯
Project directories	⎯⎯	⎯⎯	⎯⎯⎯⎯⎯
Controlling Section			
Inspection reports	⎯⎯	⎯⎯	⎯⎯⎯⎯⎯
Daily time records	⎯⎯	⎯⎯	⎯⎯⎯⎯⎯
Supervisor reports	⎯⎯	⎯⎯	⎯⎯⎯⎯⎯
Change orders	⎯⎯	⎯⎯	⎯⎯⎯⎯⎯
Status reports	⎯⎯	⎯⎯	⎯⎯⎯⎯⎯
Project manager's daily construction reports	⎯⎯	⎯⎯	⎯⎯⎯⎯⎯
Labor report forms	⎯⎯	⎯⎯	⎯⎯⎯⎯⎯
Miscellaneous Section			
Contracts	⎯⎯	⎯⎯	⎯⎯⎯⎯⎯
Memoranda	⎯⎯	⎯⎯	⎯⎯⎯⎯⎯
Minutes of meetings	⎯⎯	⎯⎯	⎯⎯⎯⎯⎯
Other correspondence	⎯⎯	⎯⎯	⎯⎯⎯⎯⎯

SAMPLE MATRIX FOR DETERMINING CRITICAL PATH

Activity	Earliest Start Equal to Latest Start?	Earliest Finish Equal to Latest Finish?	Duration Equals Latest Finish Time Minus Earliest Start Time?
Clear Site	Yes	Yes	Yes
Prepare Access to Roads	No	No	No
Conduct Survey	Yes	Yes	Yes
Rough Grade	Yes	Yes	Yes
Transport Tools to Site	Yes	Yes	Yes
Transport Huts to Site	No	No	No
Prepare Concrete Mixing Area	No	No	No
Transport Crane to Site	Yes	Yes	Yes
Assemble Crane	Yes	Yes	Yes
Excavate for Sewer	Yes	Yes	Yes

DAILY TIME REPORT

Project Title/No. _____						Date _____	
Location _____							
Activity _____				_____			
(Title)				(i–j)			

Employee Badge No.	Employee Name	Time		Hours			Remarks
		Start	End	Regular	Overtime	Total	

(Preparer's Signature)

DAILY CONSTRUCTION REPORT

Project Title/No. _____   Date _____

Temperature _____ A.M. _____P.M.

Weather _____

Activity Description	i–j	Labor					Subcontractor
		Supervisors	Mechanics	Laborers	Other	Total	

REMARKS

_____
(Preparer's Signature)

DAILY MATERIAL REPORT

Project Title/No. _____   Date _____
Location _____

How Delivered	Invoice No.	Material Description	Delivered by Whom	Cost per Unit	Quantity	Tax	Remarks

DAILY EQUIPMENT REPORT

Project Title/No. _____ Date _____
Location _____

Activity	i–j	Kind of Work Done	Company	Hours	Rate	Total Cost

REMARKS

_____
(Preparer's Signature)

CHECKLIST FOR SELECTING PROJECT MANAGEMENT SOFTWARE

	Yes	No
Network Diagrams	_____	_____
Noncritical Path	_____	_____
Critical Path	_____	_____
Precedence Logic	_____	_____
i–j Designations	_____	_____
Events or Milestones	_____	_____
Float	_____	_____
Early Start Date	_____	_____
Early Finish Date	_____	_____
Late Start Date	_____	_____
Late Finish Date	_____	_____
Activity Name	_____	_____
Add an Activity	_____	_____
Delete an Activity	_____	_____
Link Activities Together	_____	_____
Change Task Priority	_____	_____
Gantt Chart	_____	_____
Noncritical Activity Indicator	_____	_____
Critical Activity Indicator	_____	_____
Event or Milestone Indicator	_____	_____
Delay Start Indicator	_____	_____
Time Available Indicator	_____	_____
Add an Activity	_____	_____
Delete an Activity	_____	_____
Change an Activity	_____	_____
Link Activities	_____	_____
Activity Gantt	_____	_____
Resource Gantt	_____	_____
Percent Activity Complete	_____	_____
Delay Finish Indicator	_____	_____
Phase Name	_____	_____
Activity Name	_____	_____
Calendaring	_____	_____
Add a Holiday	_____	_____
Delete a Holiday	_____	_____
Change Size of Work Week	_____	_____
Project Start Date	_____	_____
Activity Calendar	_____	_____
Resource Calendar	_____	_____

Activity Details

   Add an Activity

   Change an Activity

   Delete an Activity

   Predecessor Activity

   Next Activity

   Priority Indicator

   Early Start Date

   Early Finish Date

   Late Start Date

   Late Finish Date

   Duration

   Percent Complete

   Remaining Duration

   Actual Start Date

   Actual Finish Date

   Float

   Responsibility

   i-j Nodes

   Required Resources

   Activity Title

   Estimated Costs To-Date

   Actual Costs To-Date

Resource Details

   Estimated Costs To-Date

   Actual Costs To-Date

   Activities Per Resource

   Resource Per Activity

   Resource Cost Per Unit

   Resource Early Start

   Resource Early Finish

   Resource Late Start

   Resource Late Finish

   Resource Name

   Resource Assigned to Critical
     Path Indicator

   Fixed Cost

   Variable Cost

   Resource Leveling

Reporting Features

   Detail Level Resource Reports

   Detail Level Activity Reports

   Summary Level Resource Reports

Summary Level Activity Reports   _____   _____
Exception Reports   _____   _____
Sort Reports   _____   _____
Actual/Estimates Comparisons
   Reports   _____   _____
Customized Reports   _____   _____

Additional Considerations   _____   _____
  Ability to Add a Project   _____   _____
  Ability to Delete a Project   _____   _____
  Ability to Revise a Project   _____   _____
  Ability to Save a Project   _____   _____
  Ability to Retrieve a Project   _____   _____
  Ability to Combine Projects   _____   _____
  Maximum Number of Activities
    Number:_____   _____   _____
  Maximum Number of Resources
    Number:_____   _____   _____
  Detection of Logic Errors   _____   _____
  Develop "What If" Scenarios   _____   _____
  Adjustable Time Scales for Gantt
    and Network Charts   _____   _____
  Menu Driven   _____   _____
  Command Driven   _____   _____
  Interface with Other Application
    Programs   _____   _____

Other Features

_____   _____   _____
_____   _____   _____
_____   _____   _____
_____   _____   _____
_____   _____   _____
_____   _____   _____

REFERENCES

Adrian, James. *CM: The Construction Management Process.* Reston, Va: Reston Publishing Co., Inc., 1981.

Ahuja, Hira N. *Project management: Techniques in Planning and Controlling Construction Projects.* New York: John Wiley & Sons, Inc., 1984.

Archibald, Russell D. *Managing High-Technology Programs and Projects.* New York: John Wiley & Sons, Inc., 1976.

Benson, Ben. *Critical Path Methods in Building Construction.* Englewood Cliffs, N.J.: Prentice-Hall, 1970.

Bonney, J. B., & Frein, P. J. (Eds.) *Handbook of Construction Management and Organization.* New York: Van Nostrand Reinhold Co., 1973.

Bush, Vincent G. *Construction Management: A Handbook for Contractors, Architects, and Students.* Reston, VA: Reston Publishing Co., Inc., 1973.

Callahan, Michael T. & Hohns, Murray H. *Construction Schedules: Analysis, Evaluation, and Interpretation of Schedules in Litigation.* Charlottesville: The Miche Co., 1983.

Cleland, David I., & King, William R. *Systems Analysis and Project Management.* New York: McGraw-Hill Book Co., 1983.

Clough, Richard H. *Construction Contracting* (4th ed.). New York: John Wiley & Sons, Inc., 1981.

Clyde, James E. *Construction Inspection: A Field Guide to Practice.* New York: John Wiley & Sons, Inc., 1979.

Collier, Keith. *Managing Construction Contracts.* Reston, Va: Reston Publishing Co., 1982.

Coombs, William E., & Palmer, William J. *Construction Accounting & Financial Management* (2nd ed.). New York: McGraw-Hill Book Co., 1977.

Cushman, Robert F., & Palmer, William J. *Businessman's Guide to Construction.* Princeton, N.J.: Dow Jones Books, 1980.

Dean, Burton V. *Project Management: Methods and Studies.* New York: North-Holland, 1985.

Deatherage, George E. *Construction Office Administration.* New York: McGraw-Hill Book Co., 1964.

Fondahl, John W. *A Non-Computer Approach to the Critical Path Method for the Construction Company* (2nd ed.). Stanford: Stanford University, 1962.

Foxhall, William B. *Professional Construction Management & Project Administration.* New York: Architectural Record & The American Institute of Architects, 1972.

Gibson, John E. *Managing Research & Development.* New York: John Wiley & Sons, Inc., 1981.

Goodman, Louis J., & Love, Ralph N. (Eds.). *Project Planning and Management: An Integrated Approach.* New York: Pergamon Press, 1980.

Gorman, James E. *Simplified Guide to Construction Management.* Boston: Cahners Books Inc., 1976.

Graham, Robert J. *Project Management: Combining Technical and Behavioral Approaches for Effective Implementation.* New York: Van Nostrand Reinhold Co., 1985.

Gray, Clifford F. *Essentials of Project Management: Instructor's Manual.* New York: Petrocelli Books, Inc., 1981.

Harris, Frank, & McCaffer, Ronald. *Modern Construction Management.* London: Crosby Lockwood Staples, 1977.

Higgin, Hurth, & Jessap, Neil. *Communications in the Building Industry.* London: Tavistock Publications, 1963.

Hoepp, Joseph T., & Shaffer, L. R. *Calendar-Day CPM,* Construction Research Series No. 12, Urbana, Ill: University of Illinois, 1968.

Kavanagh, Thomas, Mullen, Frank, & O'Brien, James. *Construction Management: A Professional Approach.* New York: McGraw-Hill Book Co., 1978.

Kelley, Albert J. (edited). *New Dimensions of Project Management.* Lexington, MA, 1982.

Kerzner, Harold. *Project Management: A Systems Approach to Planning, Scheduling, and Controlling* (2nd ed.). New York: Van Nostrand Reinhold Co., 1984.

Kerzner, Harold, & Thamhain, Hans J. *Project Management for Small and Medium Size Businesses.* New York: Van Nostrand Reinhold Co., 1984.

Lock, Dennis. *Project Management* (2nd ed.). Westmead, England: Gower Press, 1977.

Lucas, Chester L. *International Construction Business Management: A Guide for Architects, Engineers, and Contractors.* New York: McGraw-Hill Book Co., 1985.

Melvine, Tom. *Practical Psychology in Construction Management.* New York: Van Nostrand Reinhold Co., 1979.

Moder, Joseph J., & Phillips, Cecil R. *Project Management with CPM and PERT* (2nd ed.). New York: Van Nostrand Reinhold Co., 1970.

O'Brien, James J. *CPM in Construction Management* (3rd ed.). New York: McGraw-Hill Book Co., 1984.

Peters, Glen. *Construction Project Management Using Small Computers.* New York: Nichols Publishing Co., 1984.

Portland Cement Association, *Administrative Practices in Concrete Construction,* New York: John Wiley & Sons, 1980.

Rauseo, Michael J. *Management Controls for Computer Processing.* New York: American Management Associations, Inc., 1970.

Roberts, Bruce. *The Project Manual.* Silver Spring, MD: Construction Industry Press, 1983.

Robertson, D. C. *Project Planning and Control: Simplified Critical Path Analysis.* London: Heywood Books, 1967.

Royer, King. *Desk Book for Construction Superintendents.* Englewood Cliffs, N.J.: Prentice-Hall, Inc., 1967.

Sackman, Harold, & Citrenbaum, L. (Eds.). *Online Planning: Towards Creative Problem-Solving.* Englewood Cliffs, N. J.: Prentice-Hall Inc., 1972.

Samaras, Thomas T., & Yensuang, Kim. *Computerized Project Management Techniques for Manufacturing and Construction Industries.* Englewood Cliffs, N. J.: Prentice-Hall Inc., 1979.

Steiner, George A., & Ryan, William G. *Industrial Project Management.* New York: The Macmillian Co., 1968.

Stewart, Donald V. *Systems Analysis and Management: Structure, Strategy, and Design.* New York: Petrocelli Books Inc., 1981.

Thomsen, Charles. B. *CM Developing, Marketing, and Delivering Construction Management Services.* New York: McGraw-Hill Book Co., 1982.

Volpe, Peter S. *Construction Management Practice.* New York: Wiley-Interscience, 1972.

Waso, Alonzo. *Construction Management and Contracting.* Englewood Cliffs, N. J.: Prentice-Hall Inc., 1972.

INDEX

There's an epidemic with 27 million victims. And no visible symptoms.

It's an epidemic of people who can't read.

Believe it or not, 27 million Americans are functionally illiterate, about one adult in five. Forty-seven million more are able to read on only the most minimal level. Together, that's almost 75 million Americans...one third of our entire population.

The solution to this problem is you...when you join the fight against illiteracy. So call the Coalition for Literacy at toll-free **1-800-228-8813** and volunteer.

Illiteracy may be an epidemic, but with a little caring from you, we can stop it.

**Volunteer Against Illiteracy.
The only degree you need
is a degree of caring.**

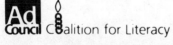